Letter Tracing

A is for

antelope

A

a

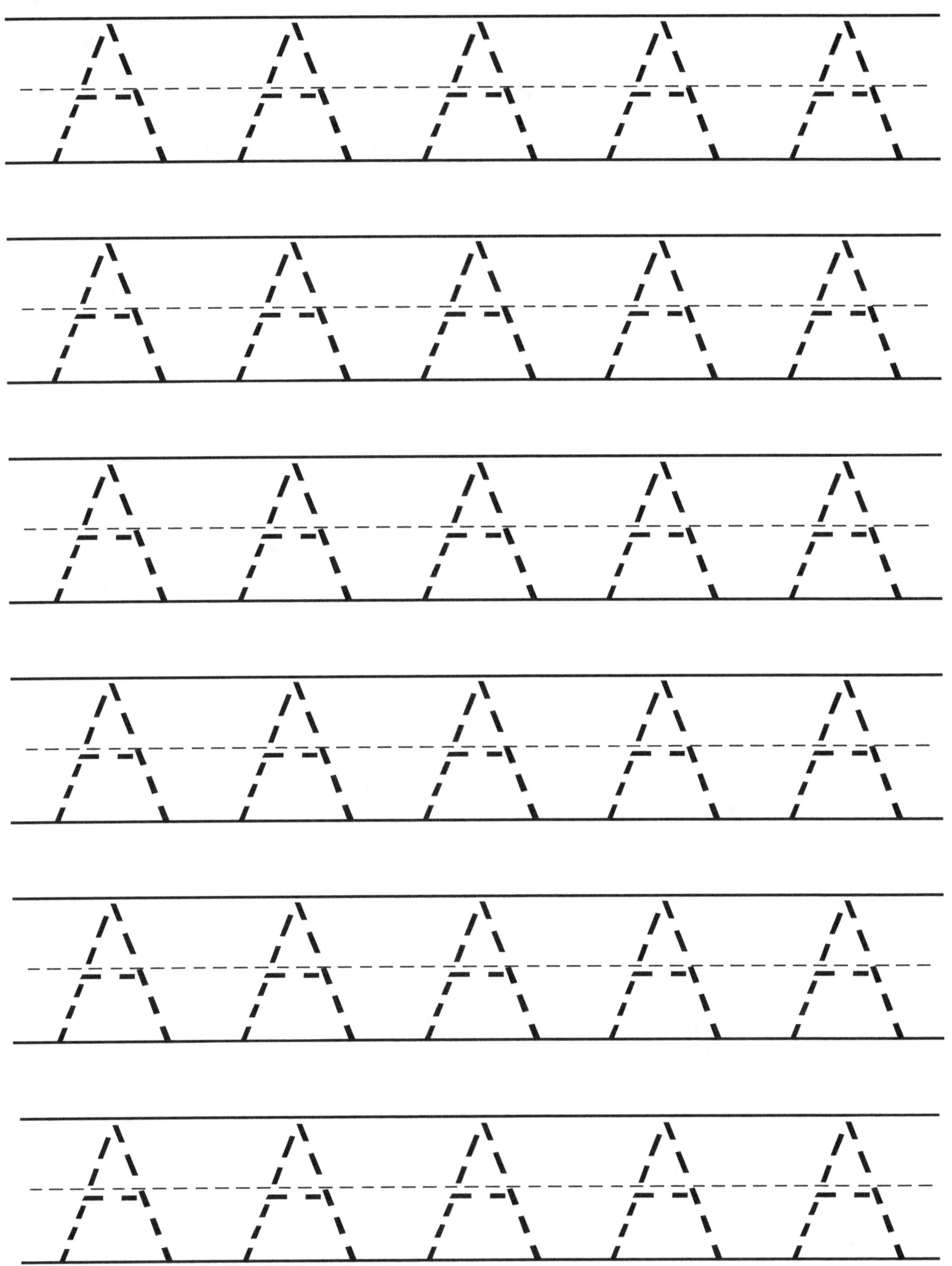

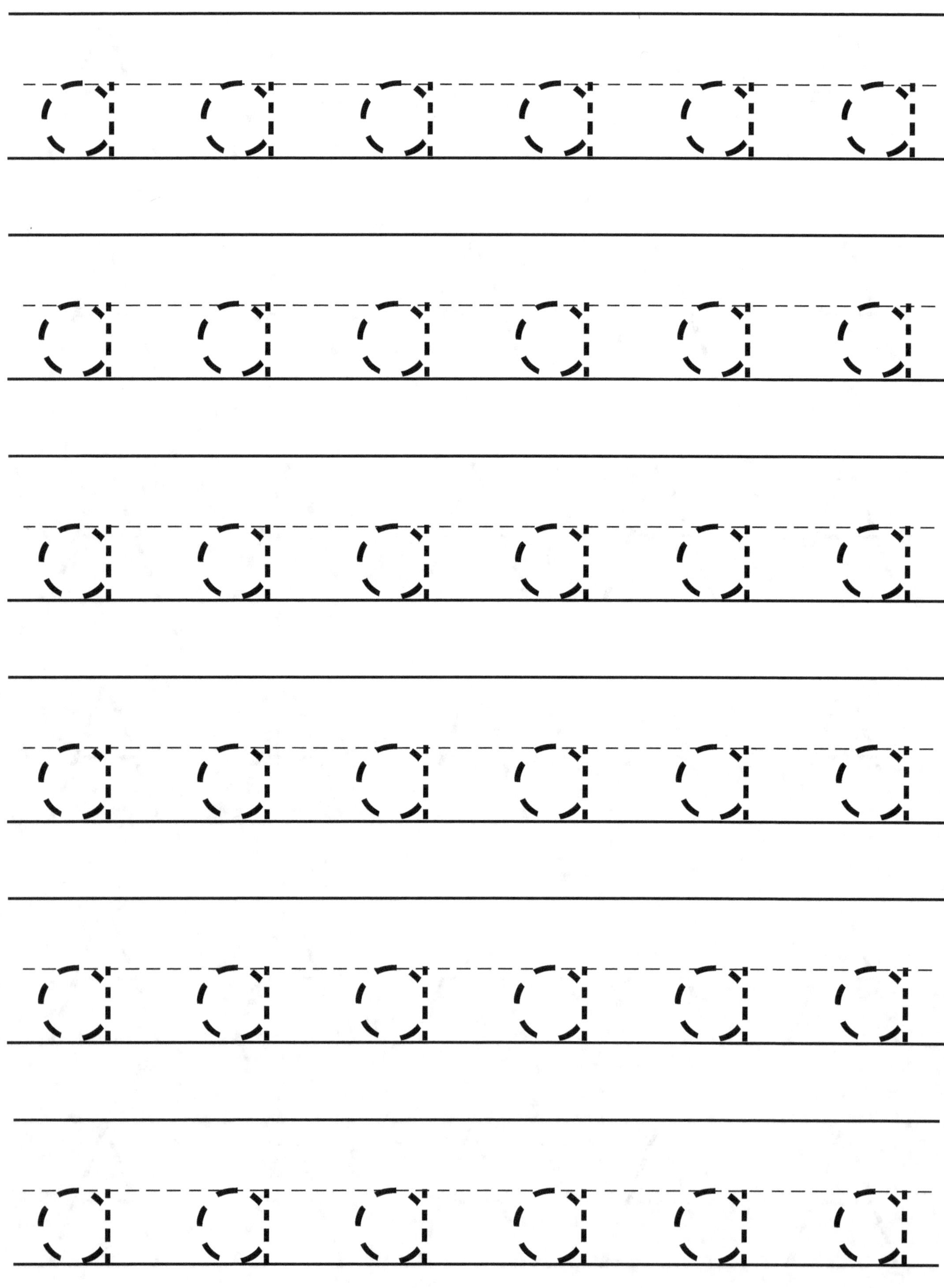

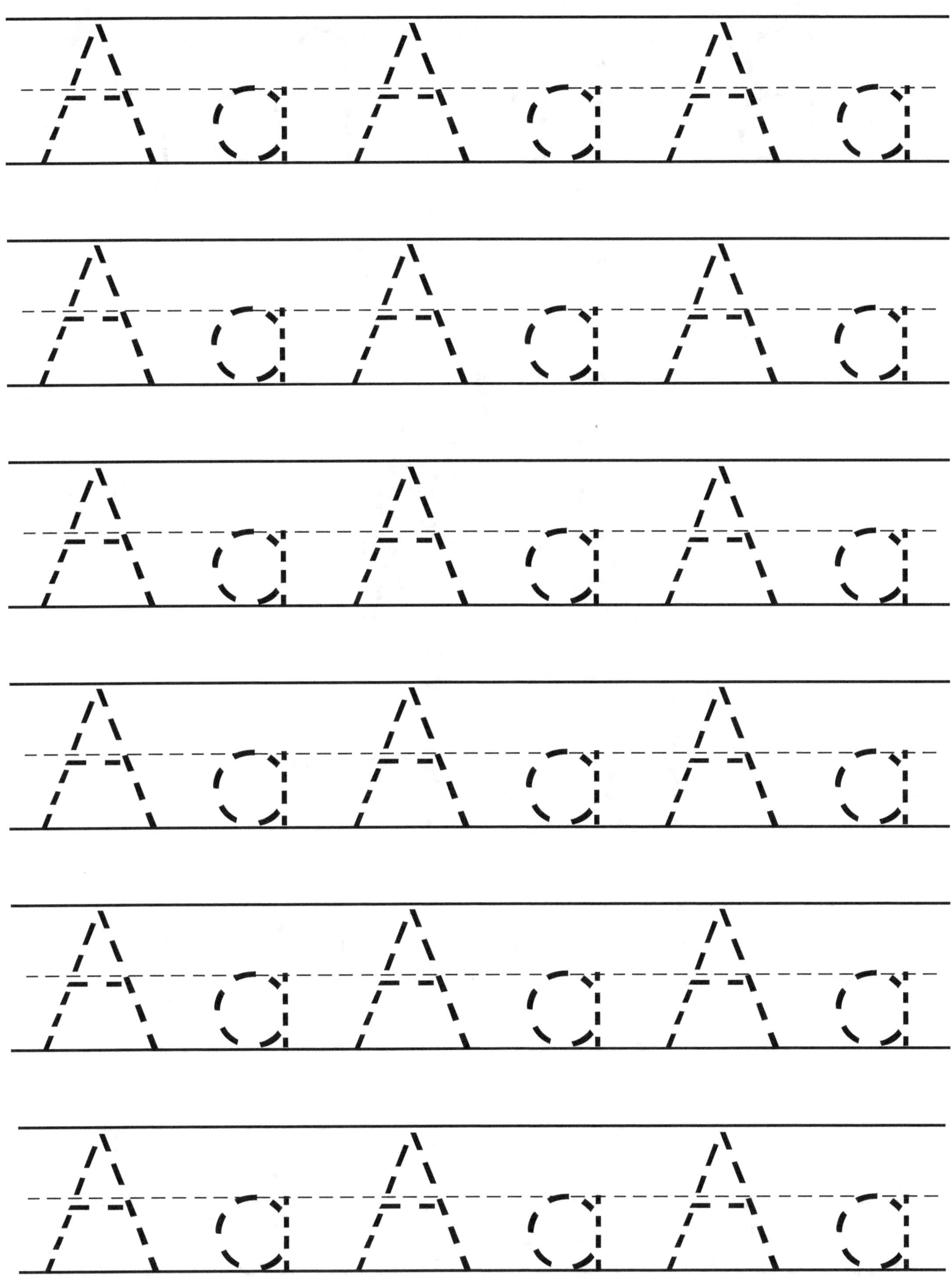

B is for

bear

B B B B B B

b b b b b b

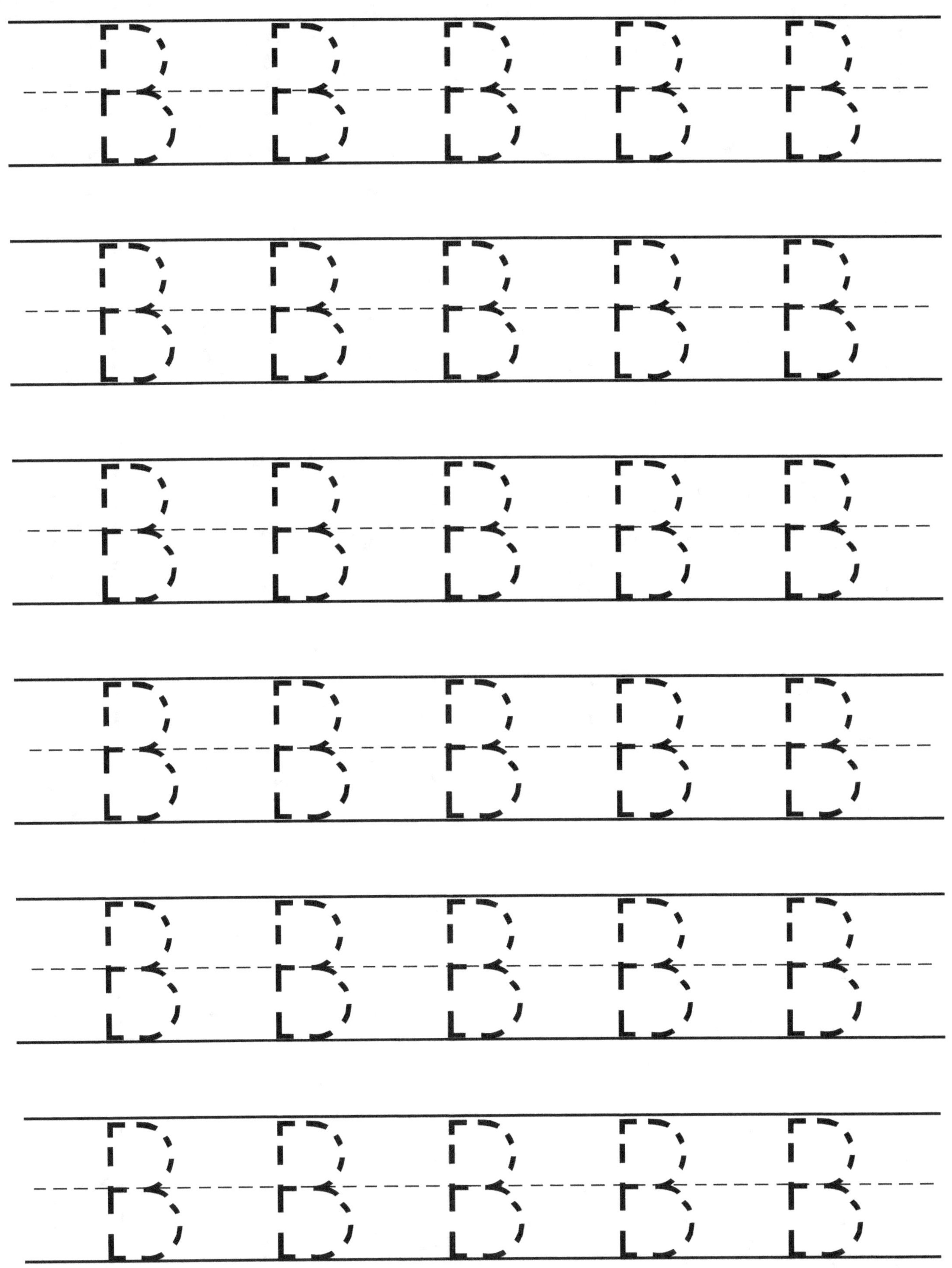

b b b b b b

b b b b b b

b b b b b b

b b b b b b

b b b b b b

b b b b b b

B b B b B b

B b B b B b

B b B b B b

B b B b B b

B b B b B b

B b B b B b

C is for

cat

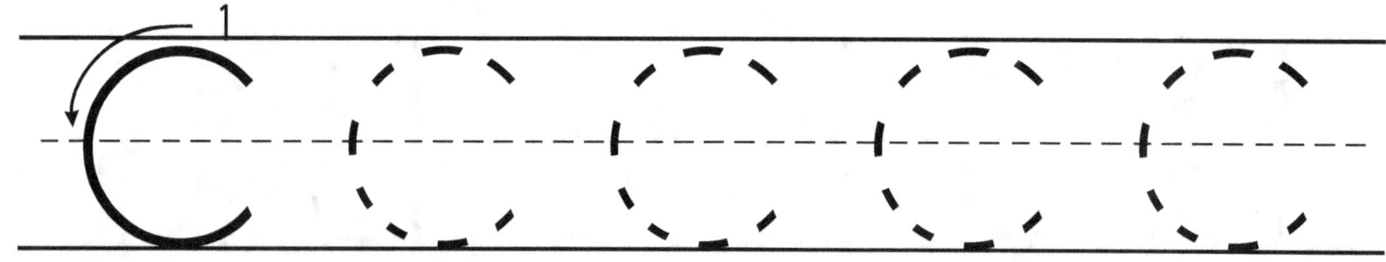

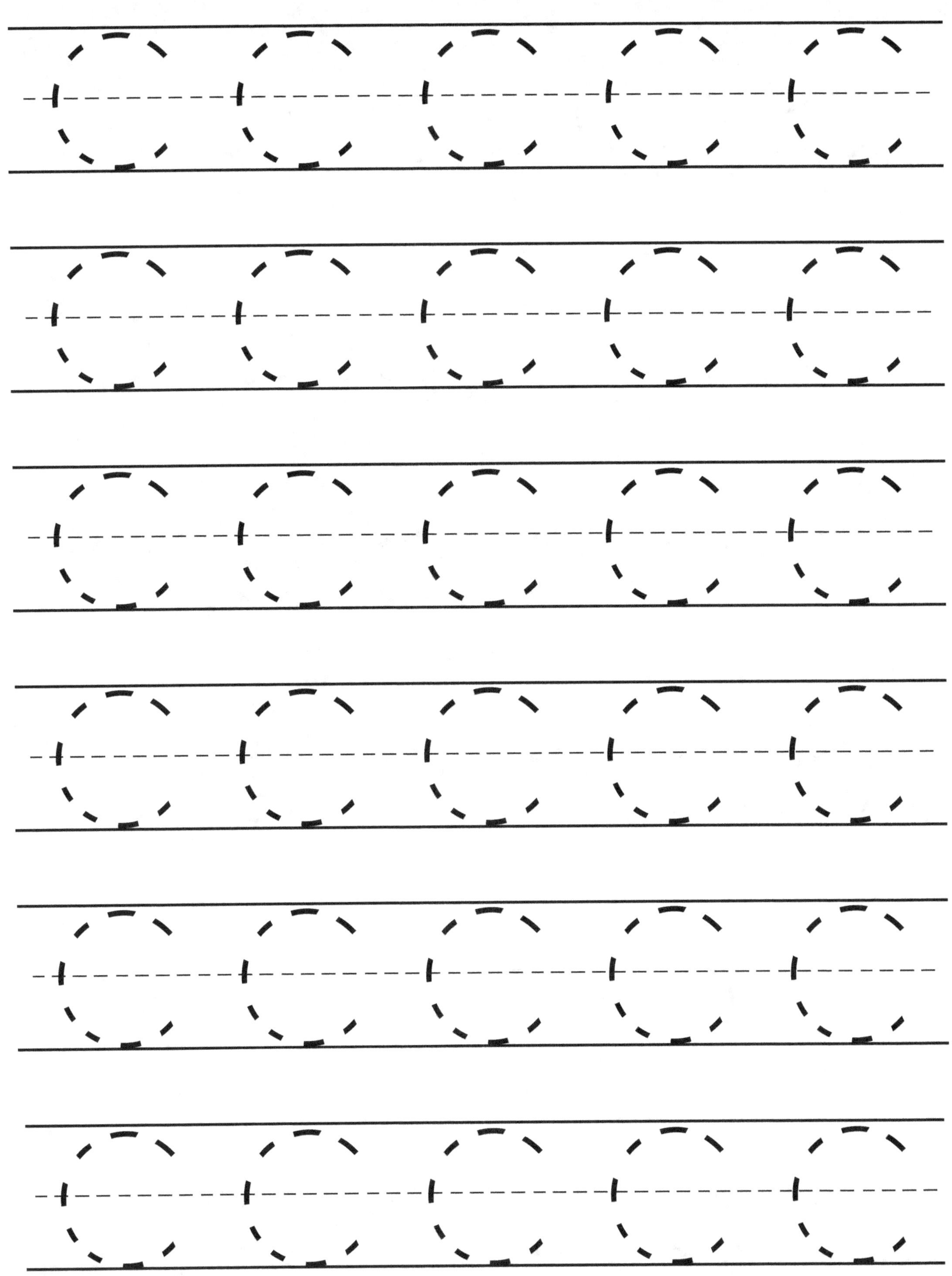

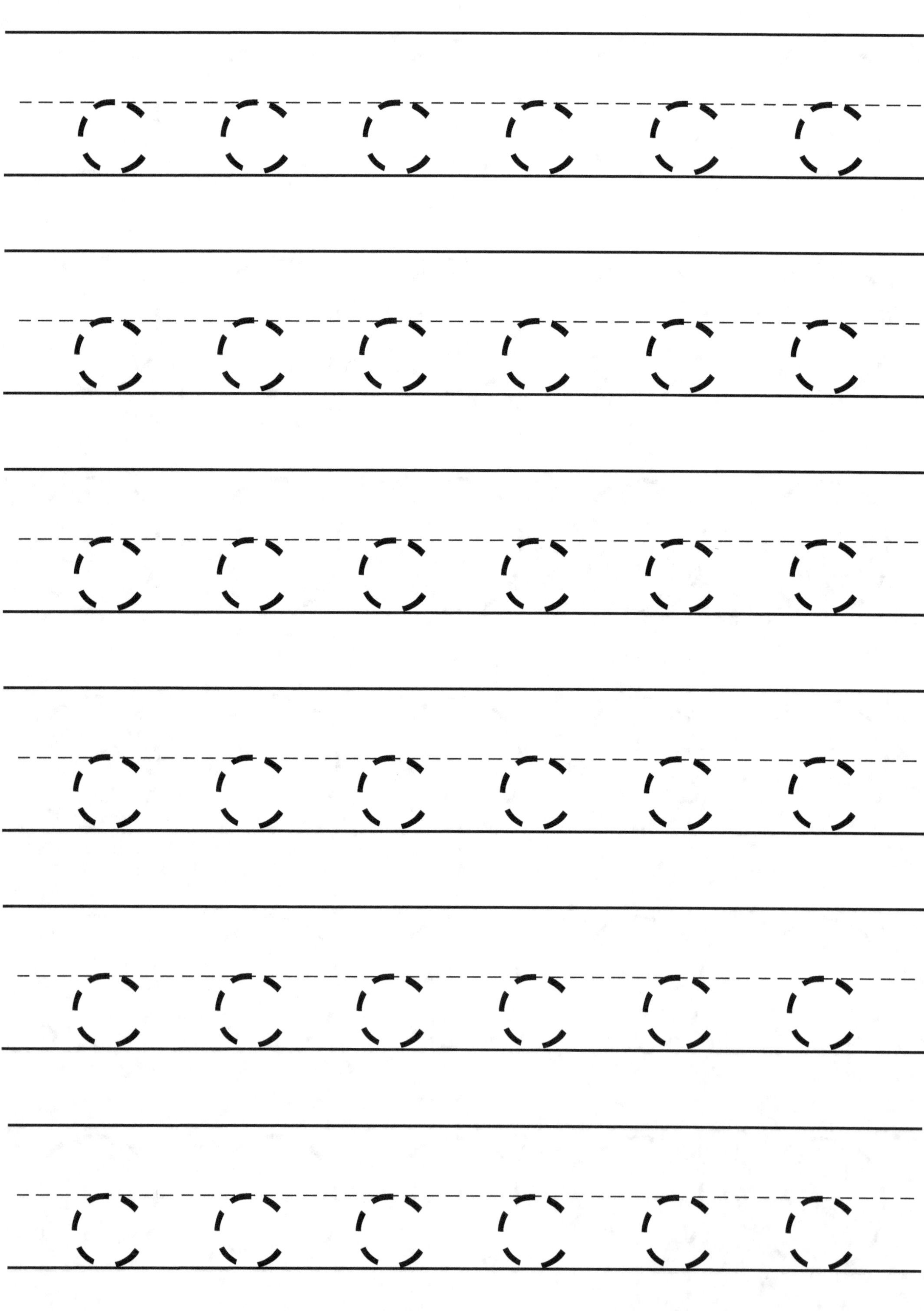

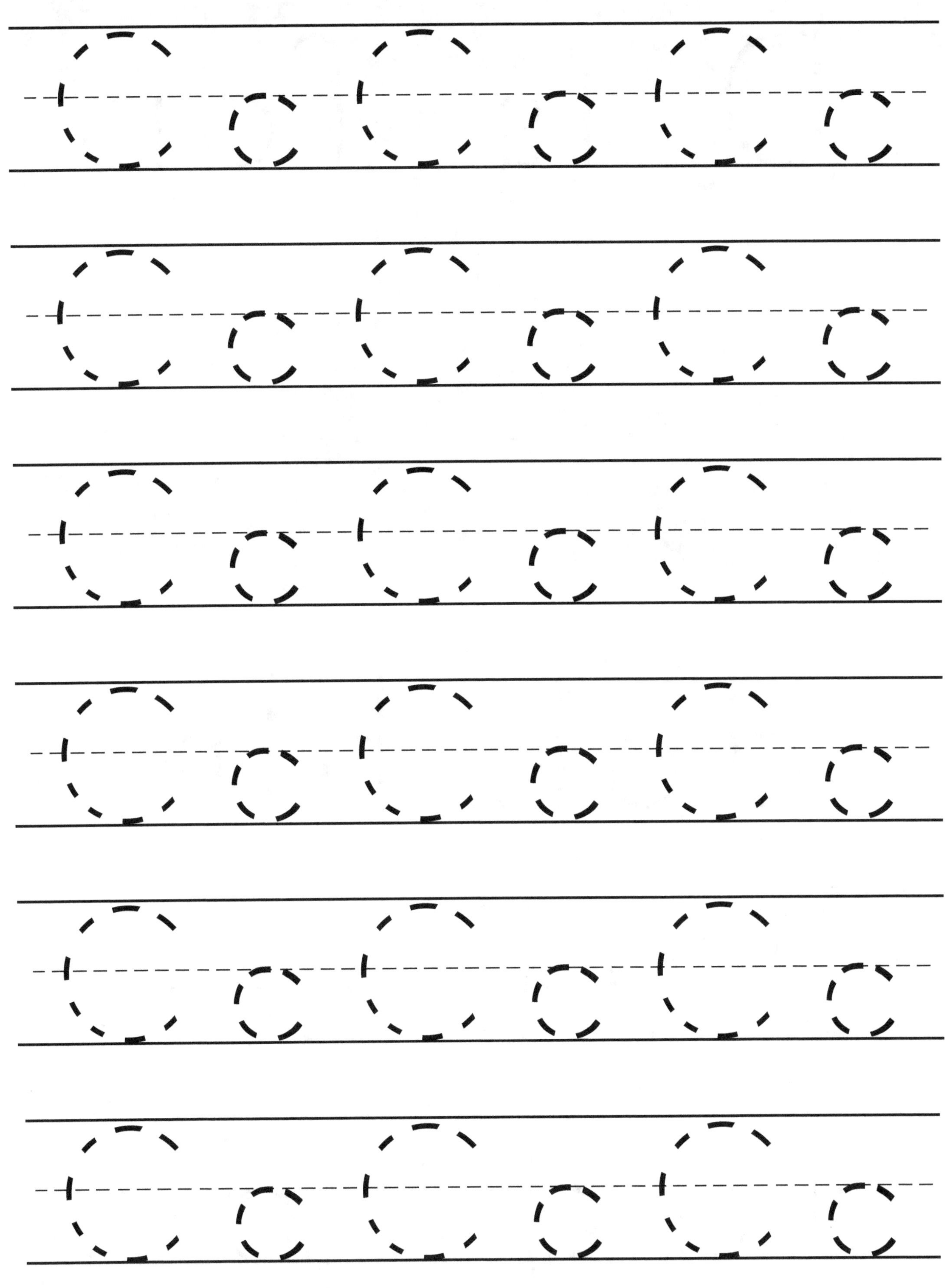

D is for

dolphin

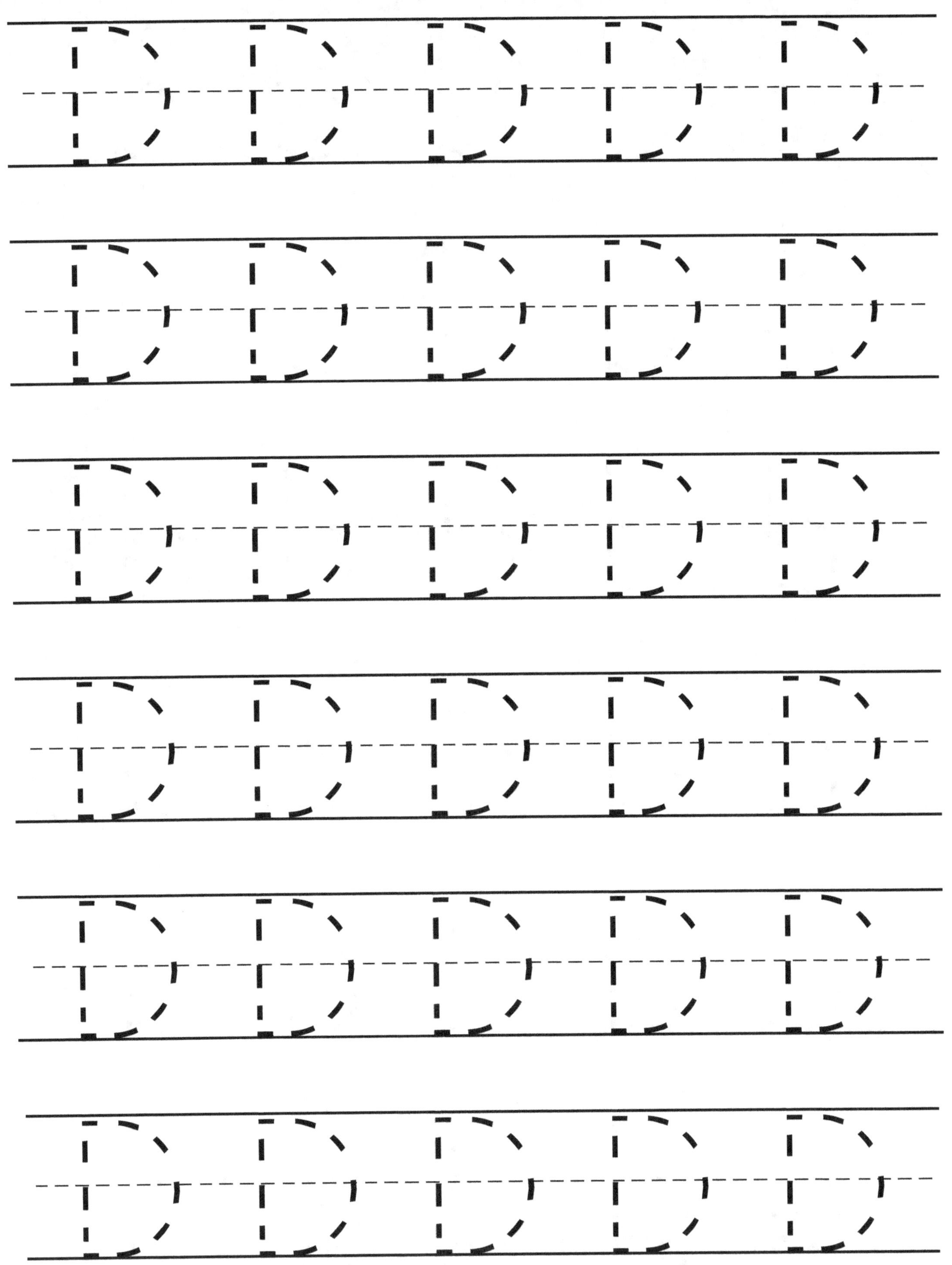

D d D d D d

D d D d D d

D d D d D d

D d D d D d

D d D d D d

D d D d D d

E is for

elephant

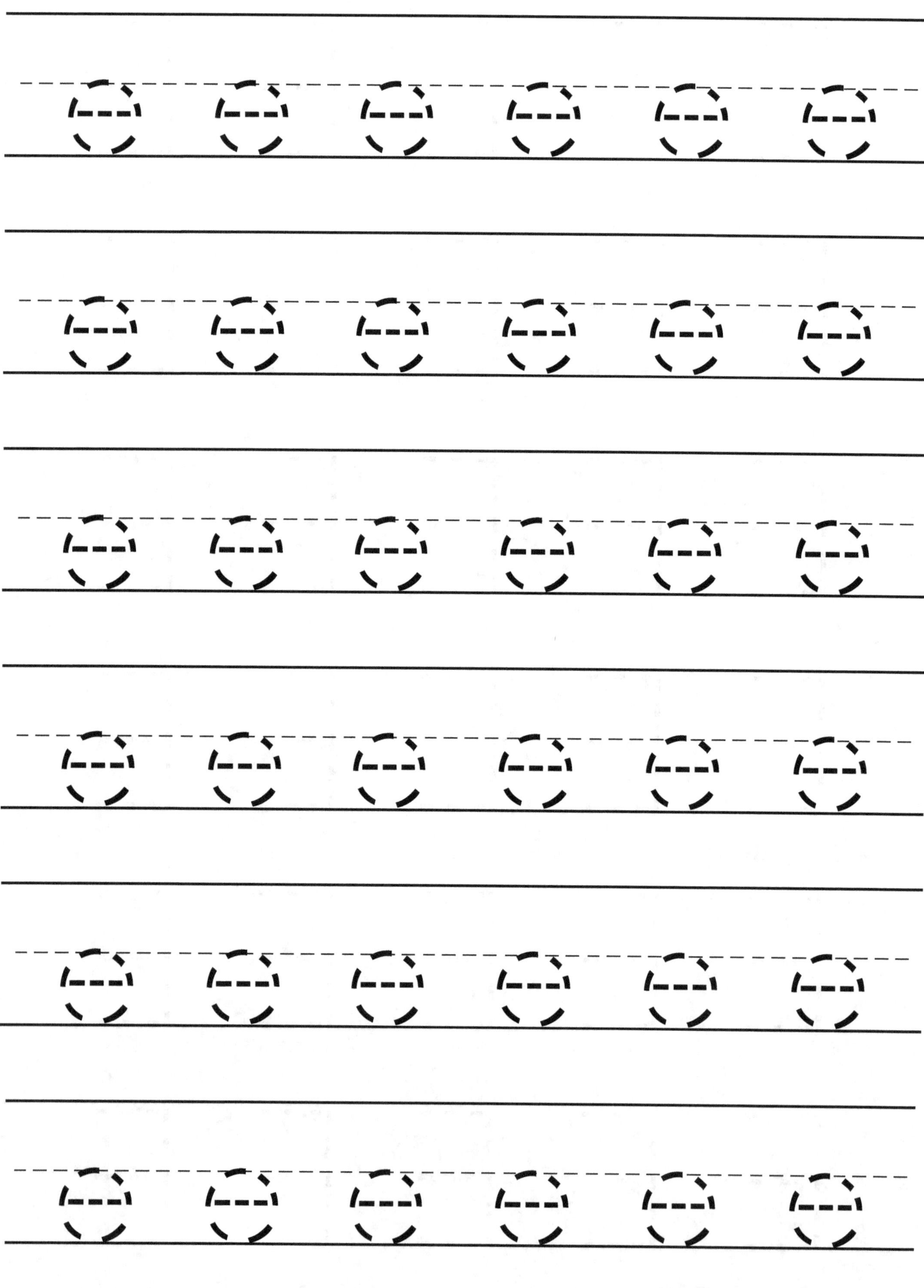

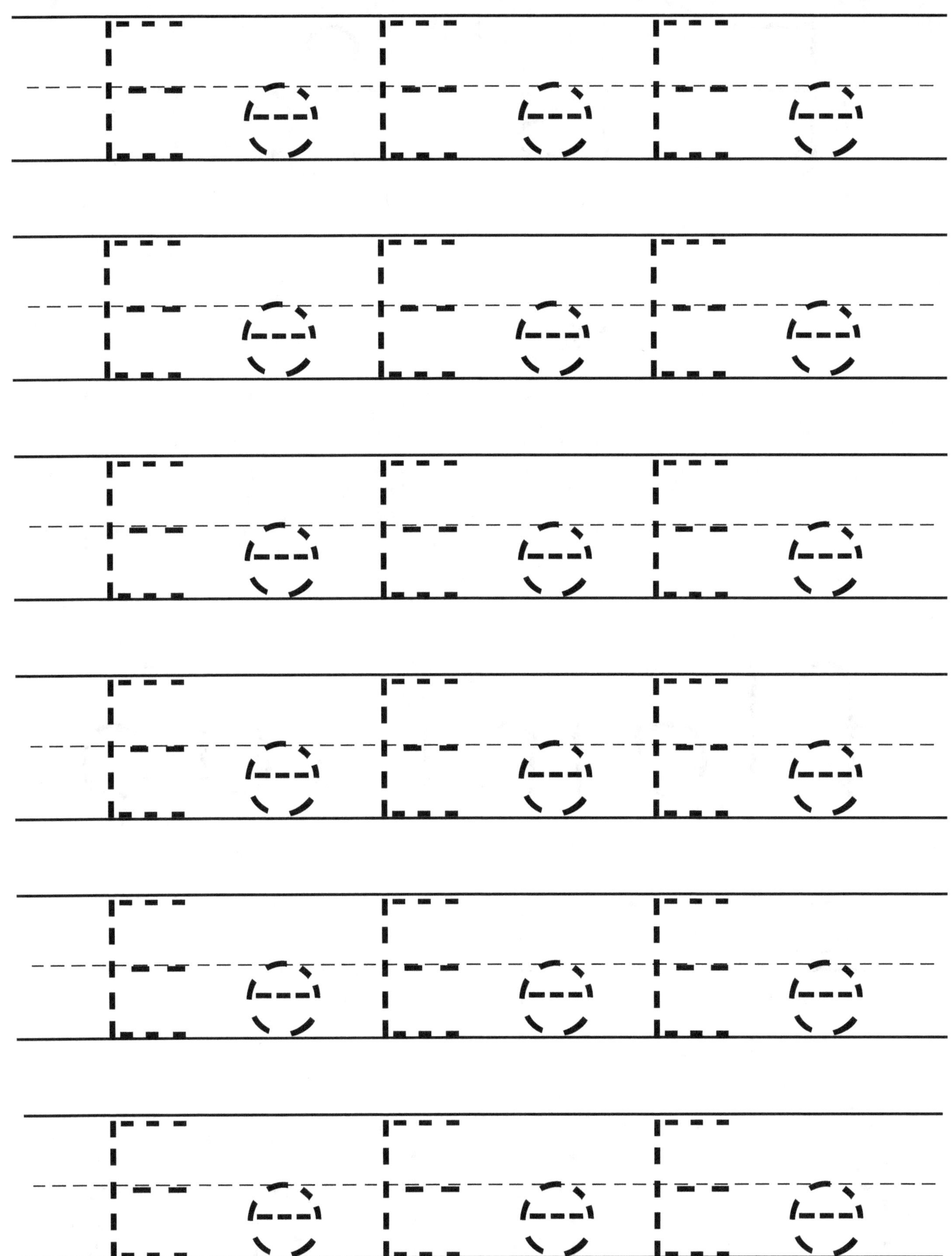

F is for

flamingo

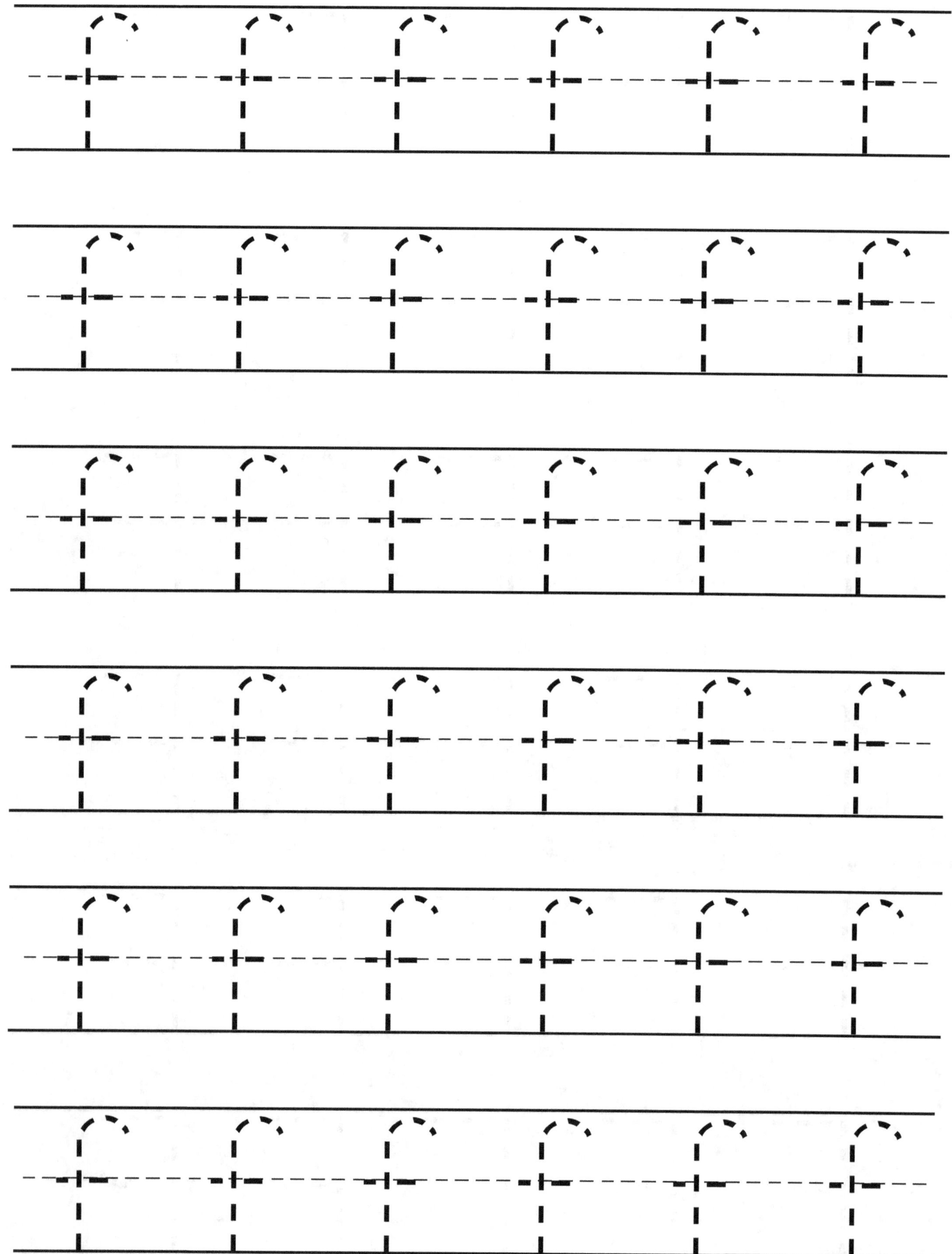

G is for

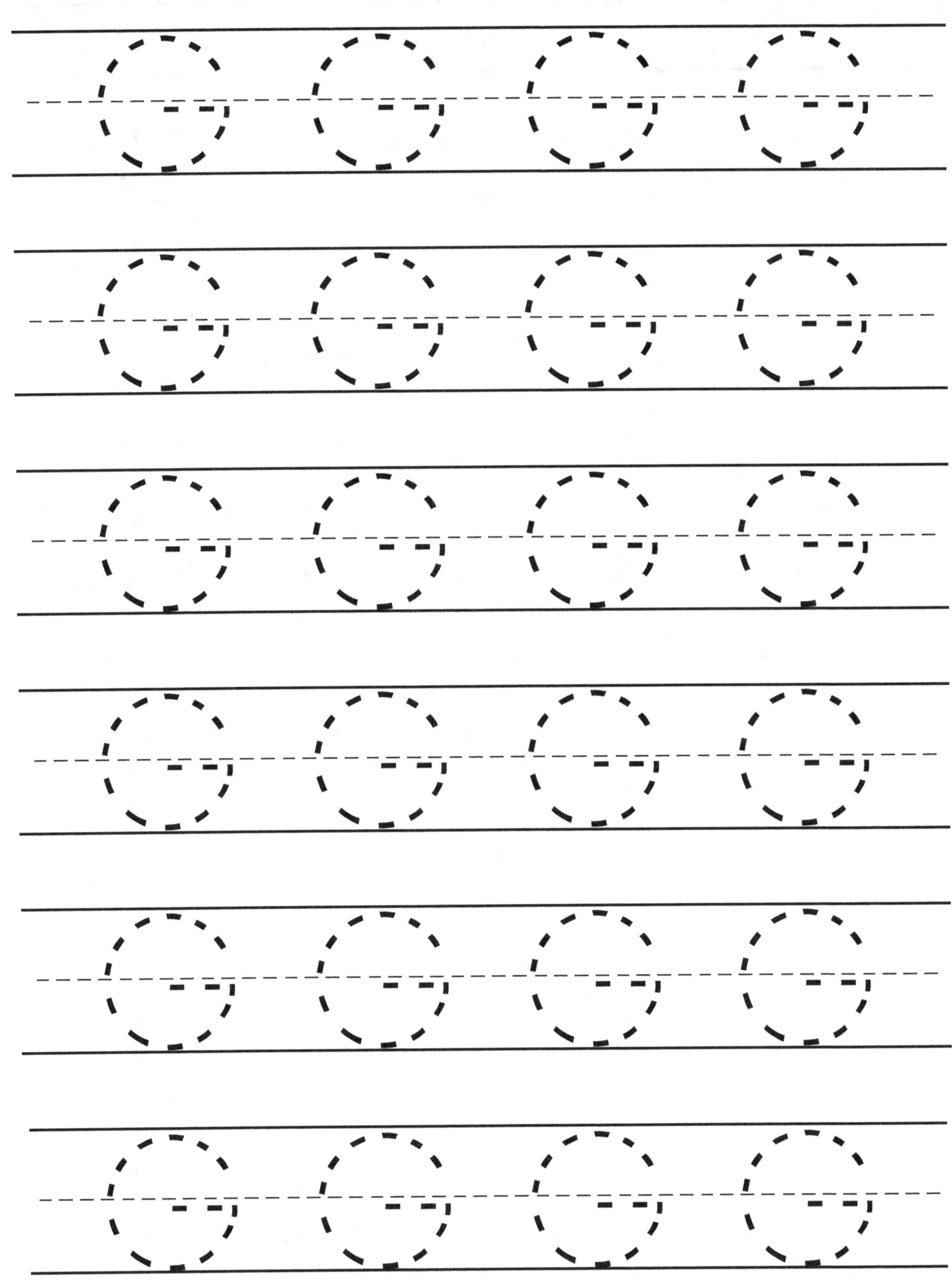

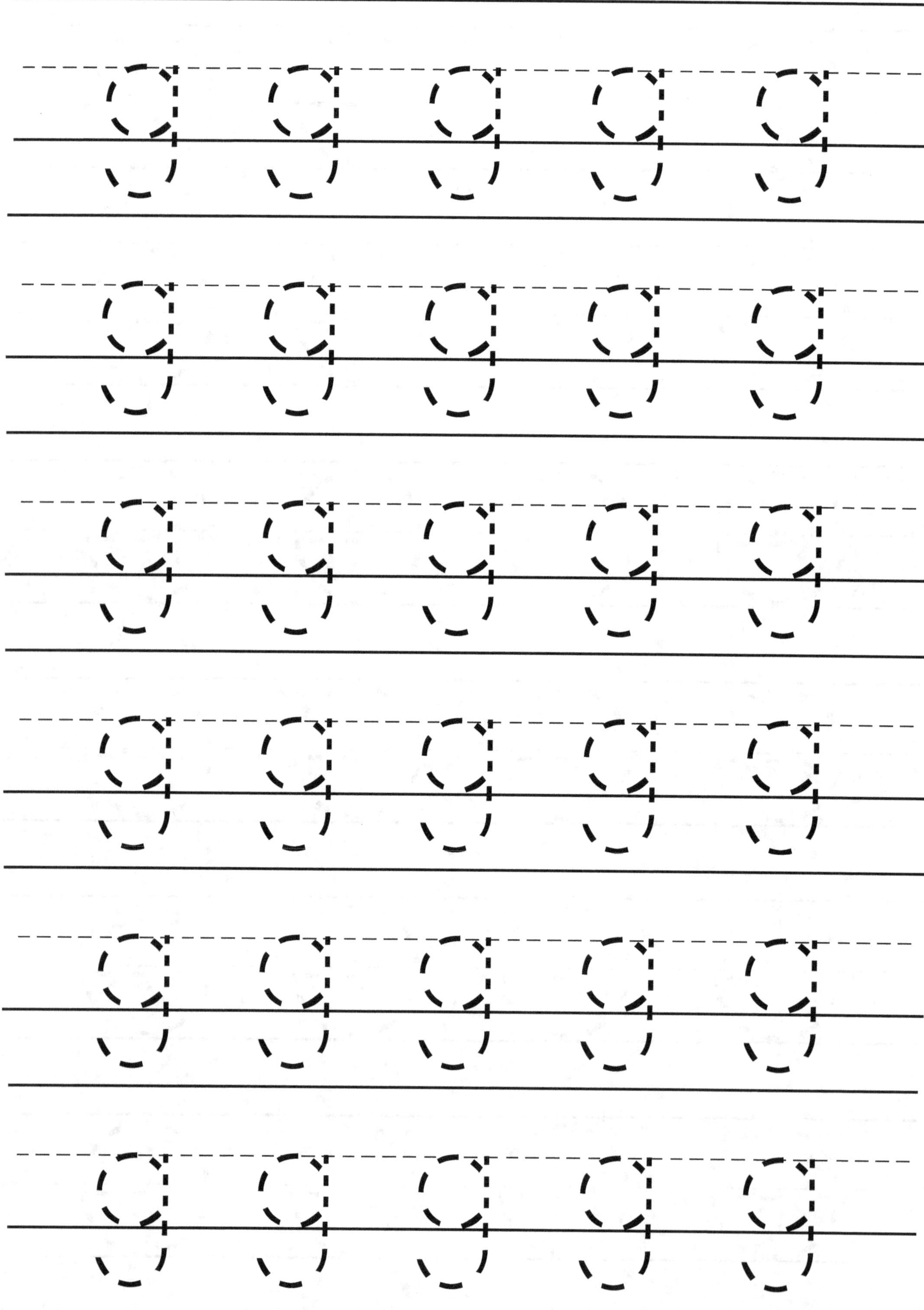

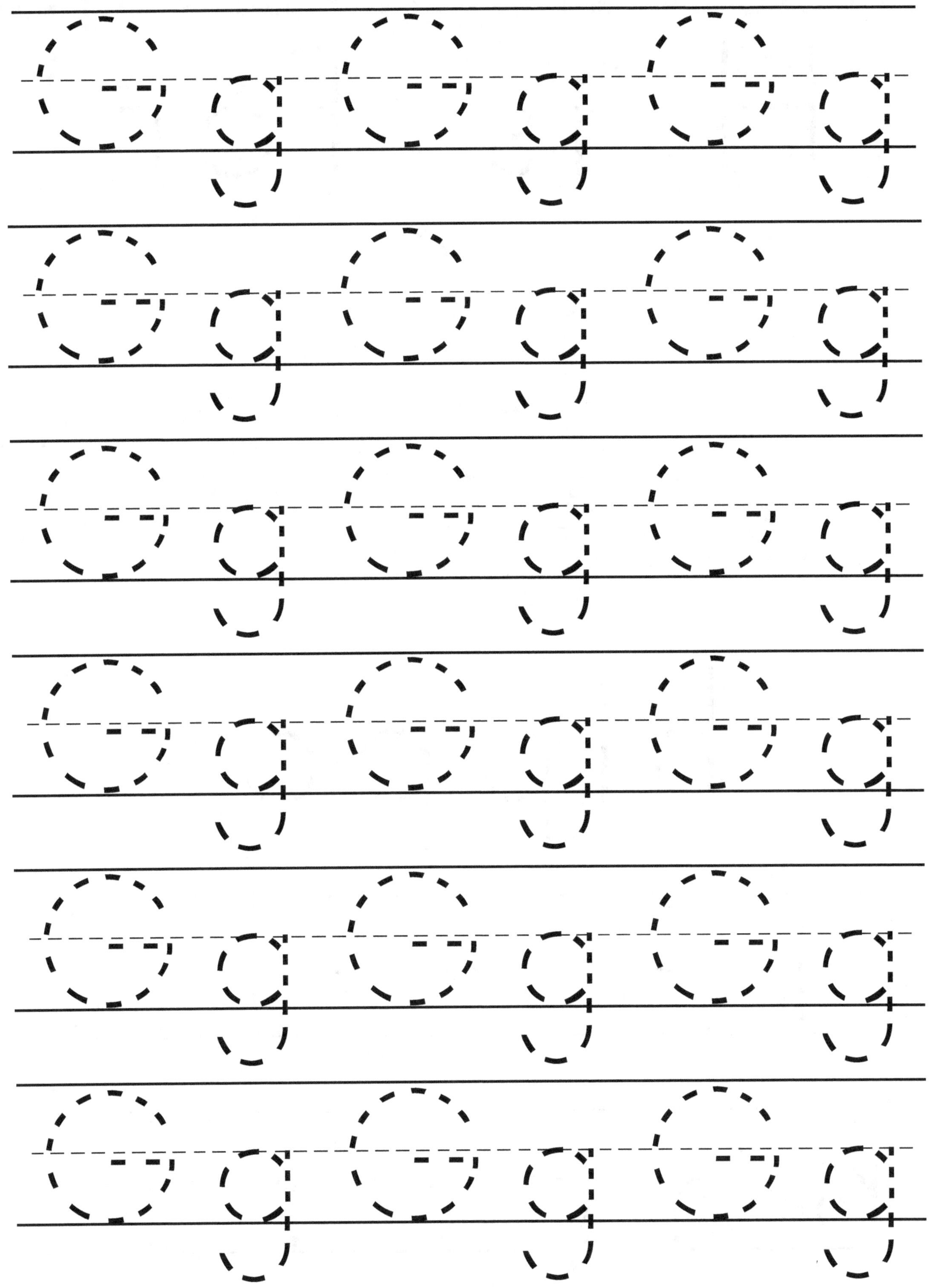

H is for

hippo

I is for

iguana

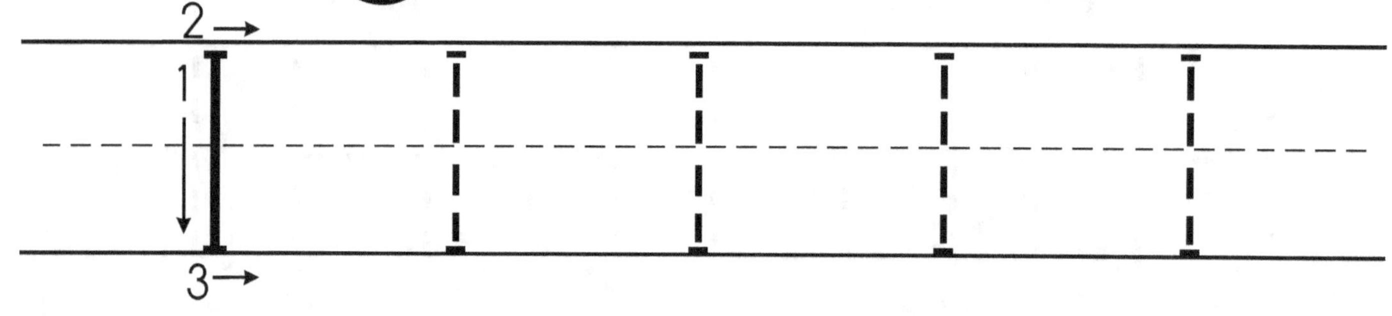

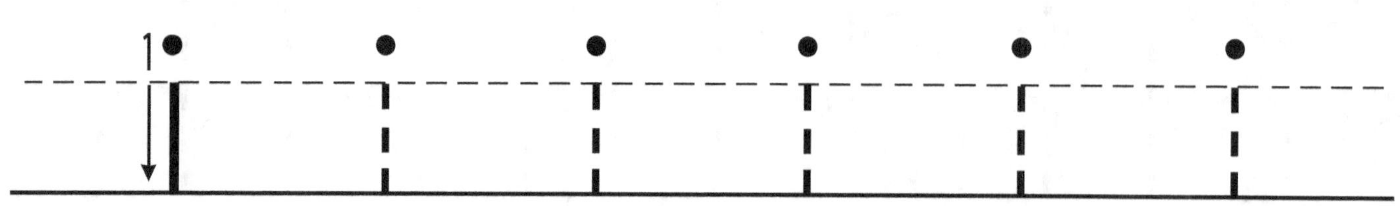

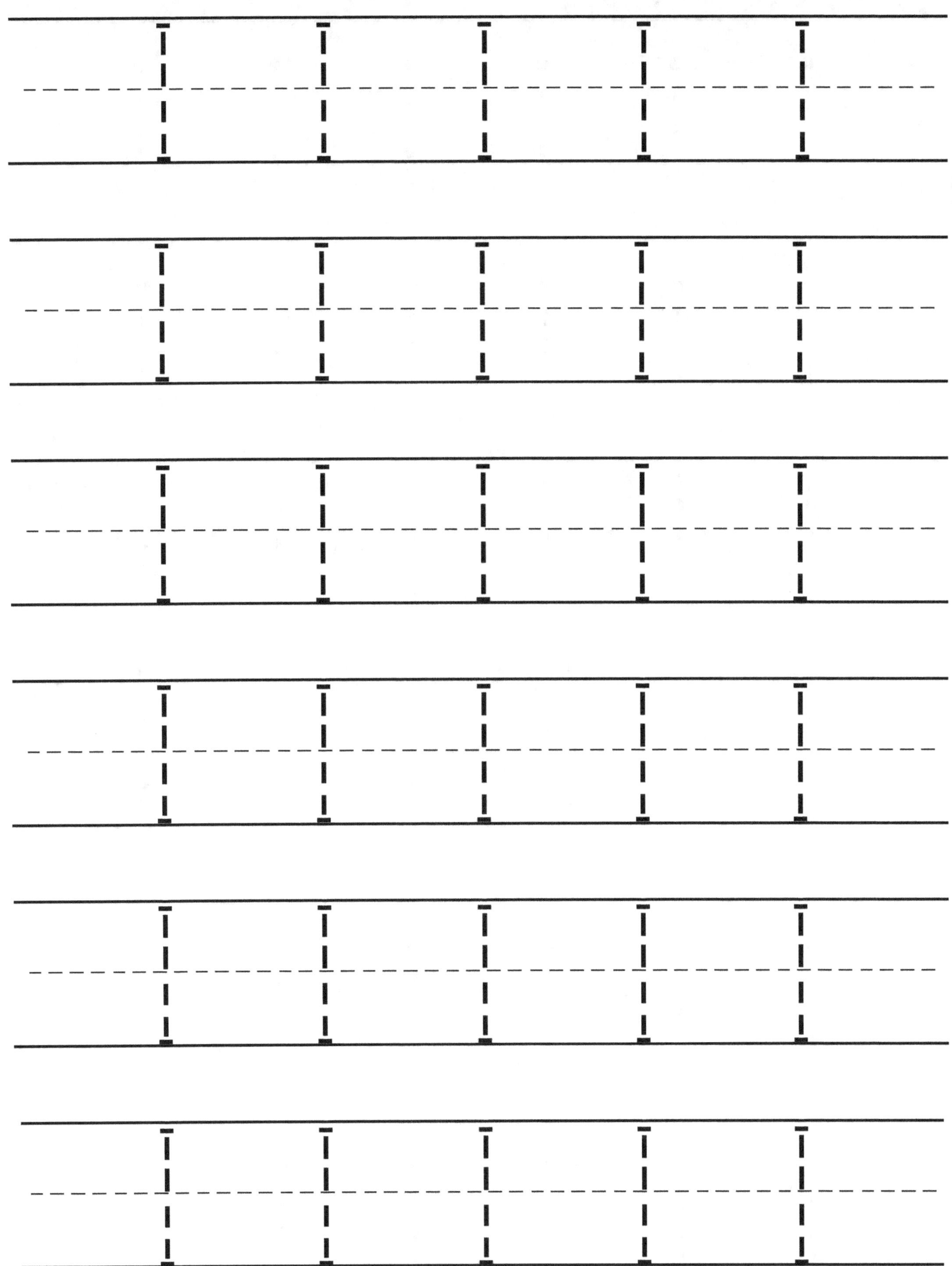

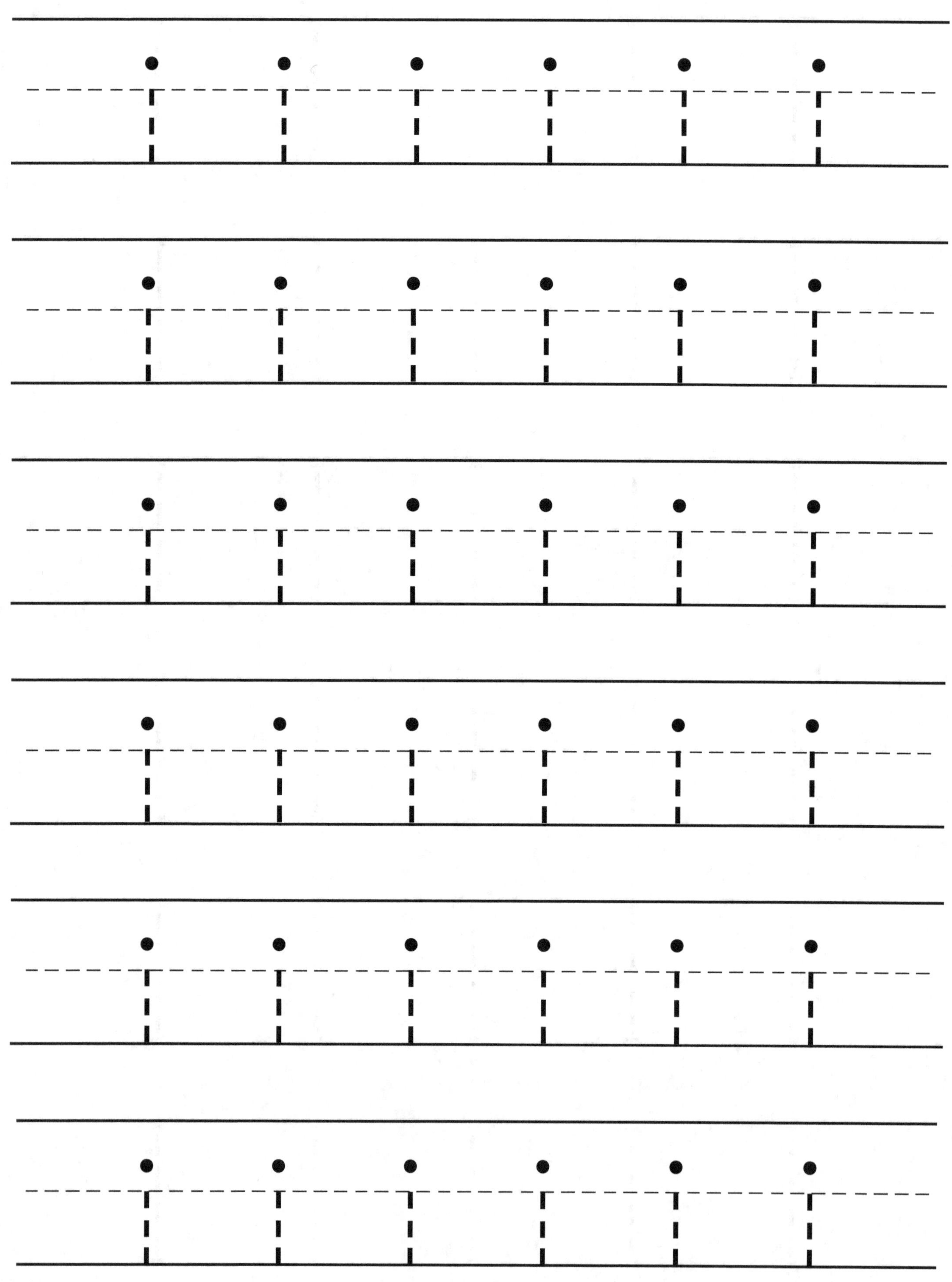

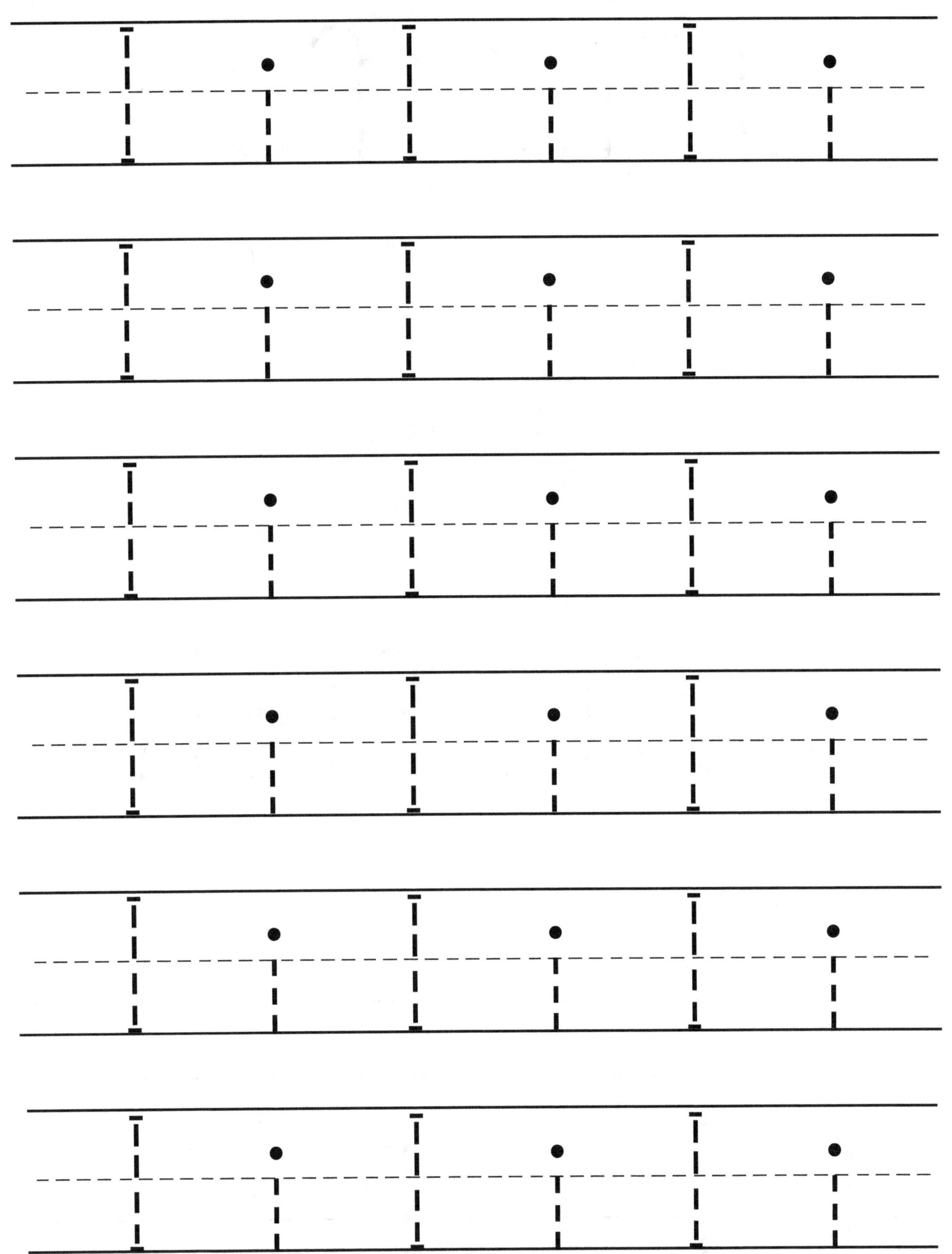

J is for

jellyfish

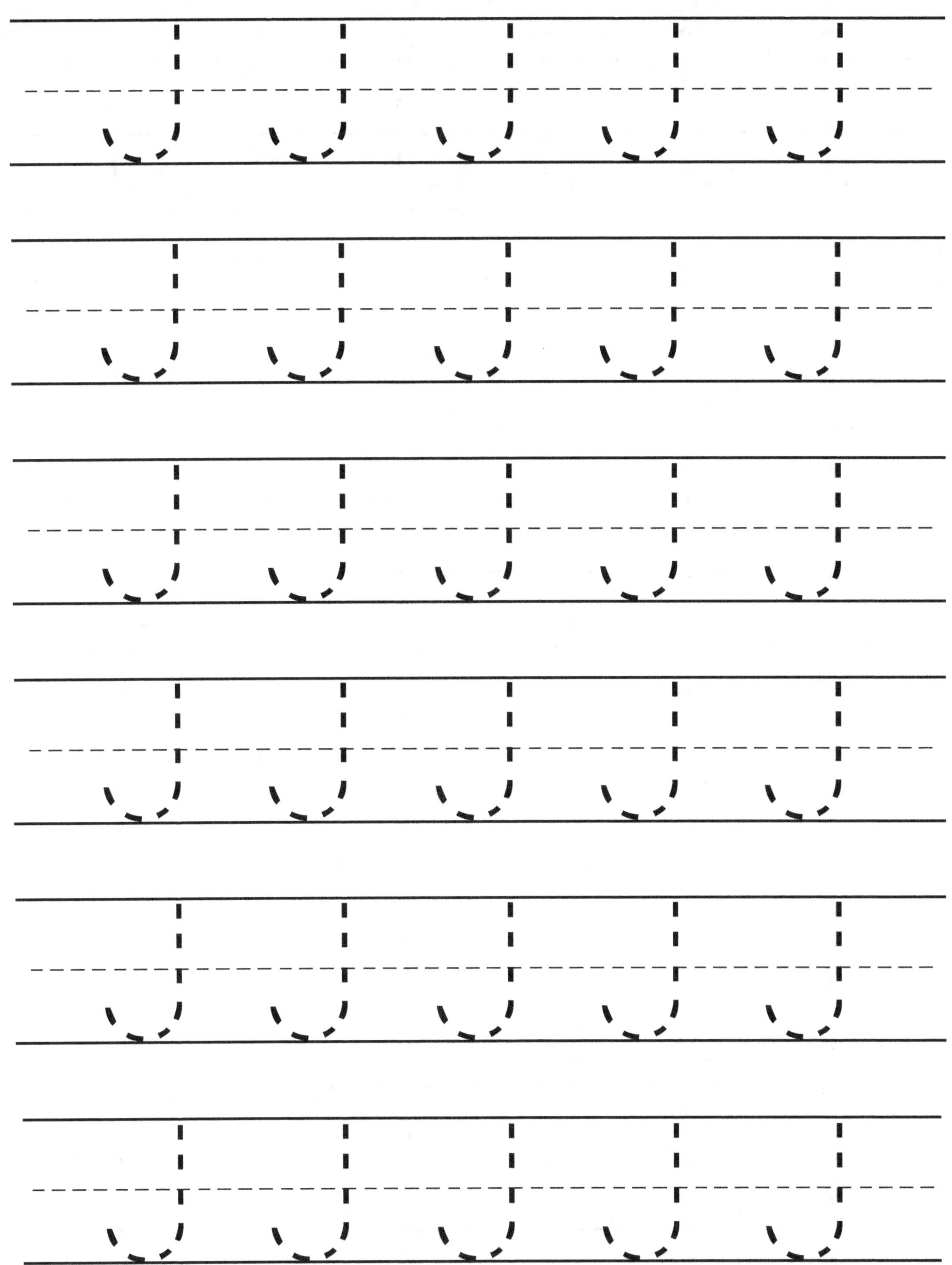

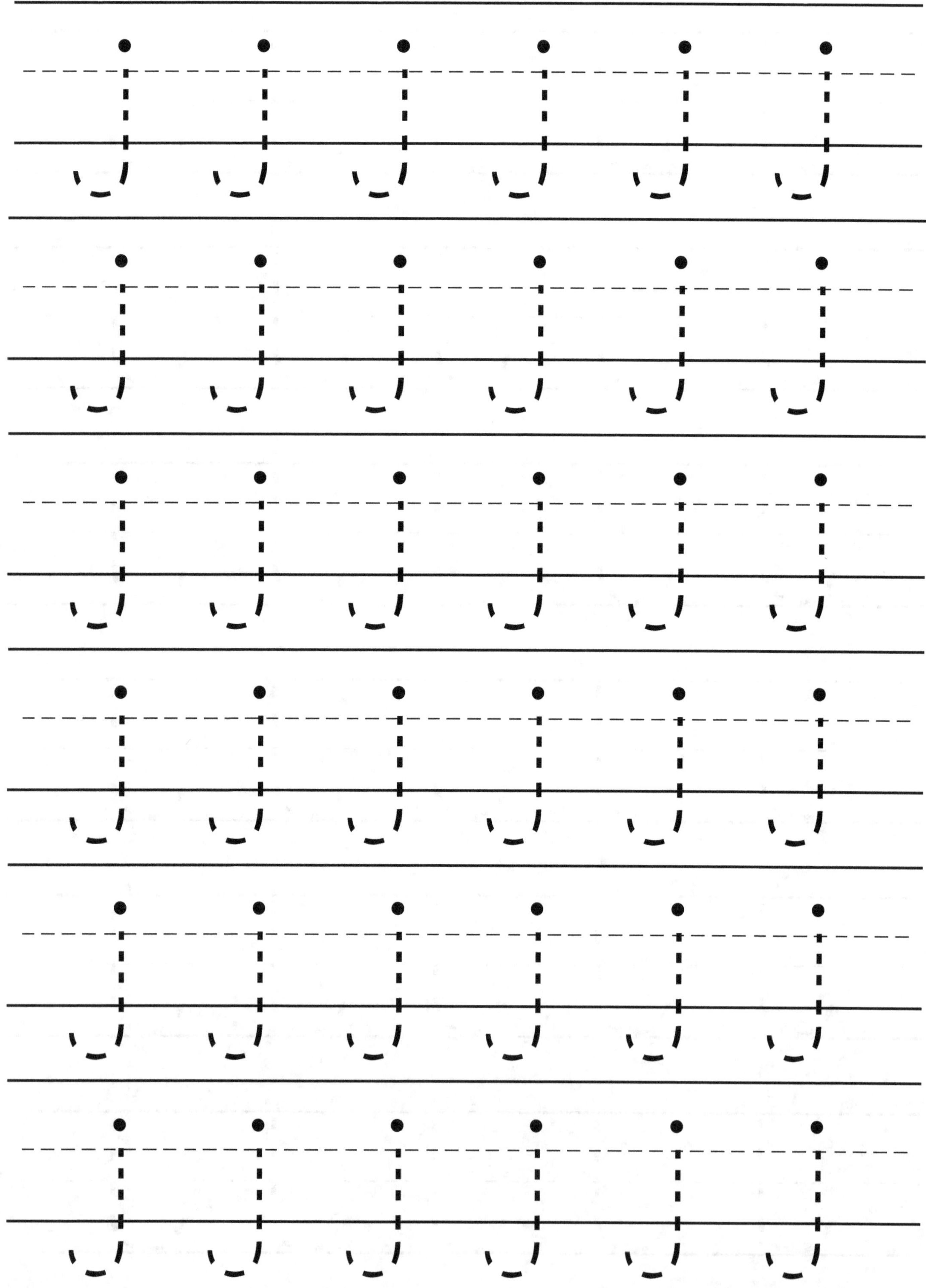

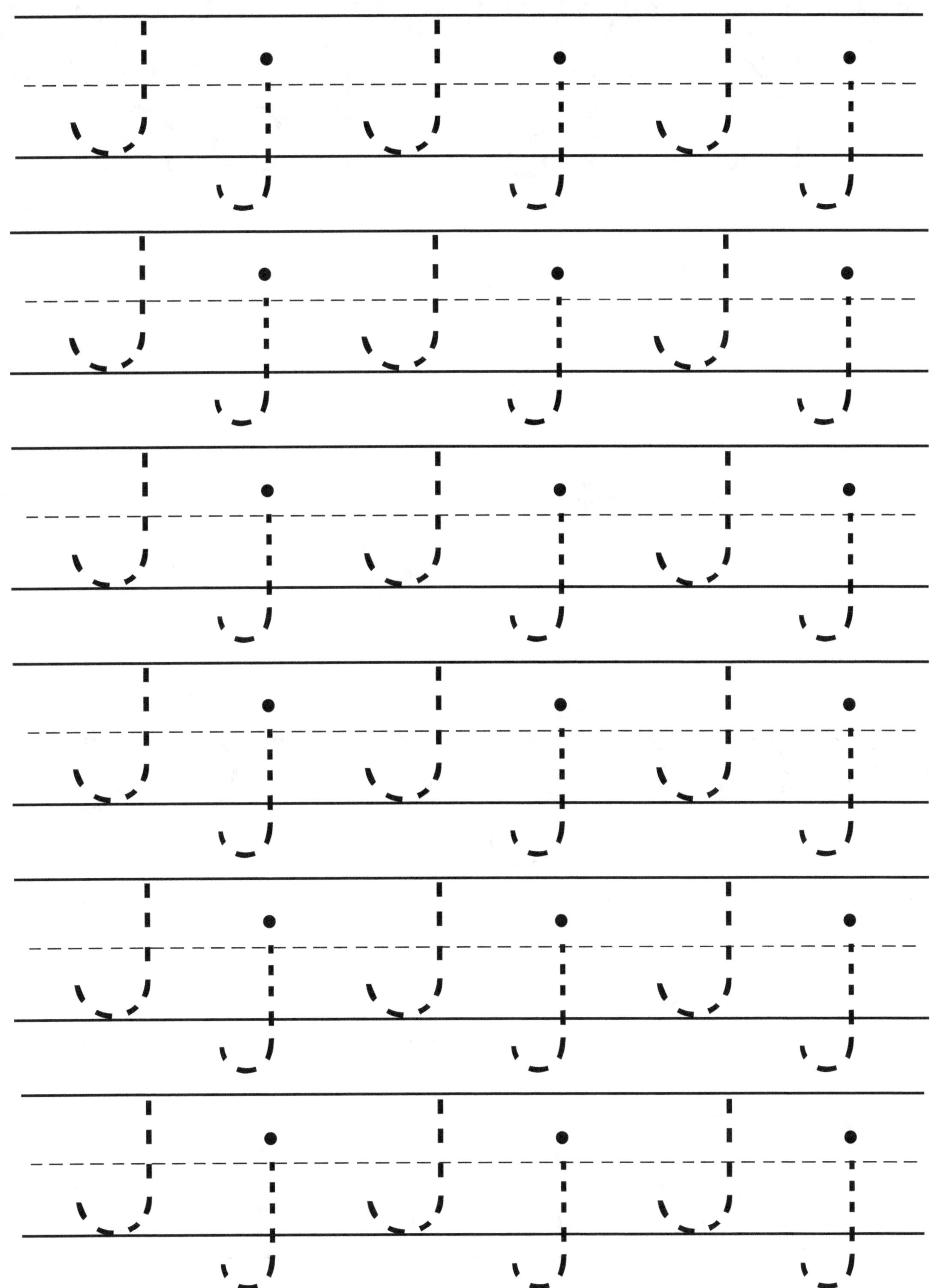

K is for

kangaroo

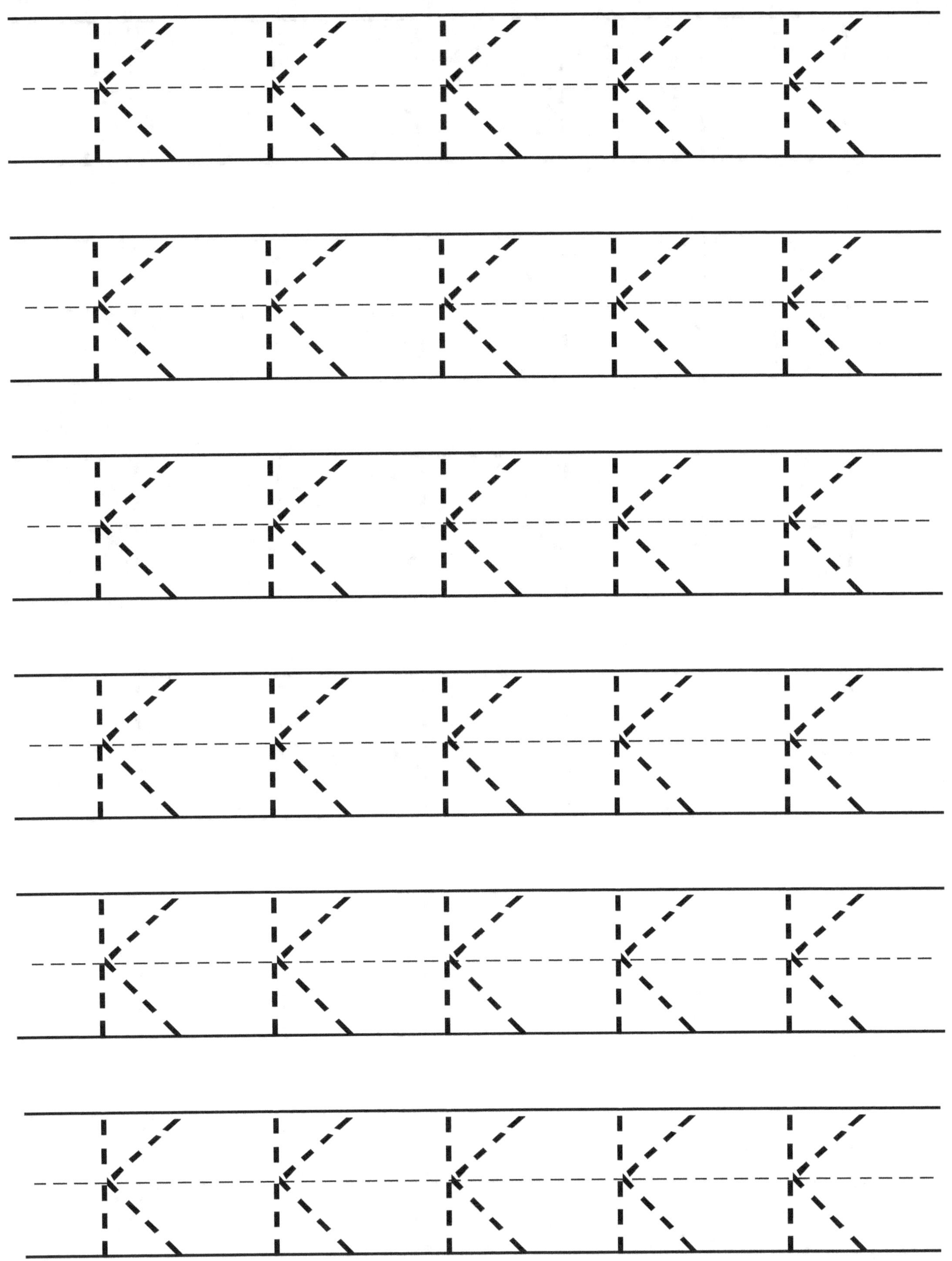

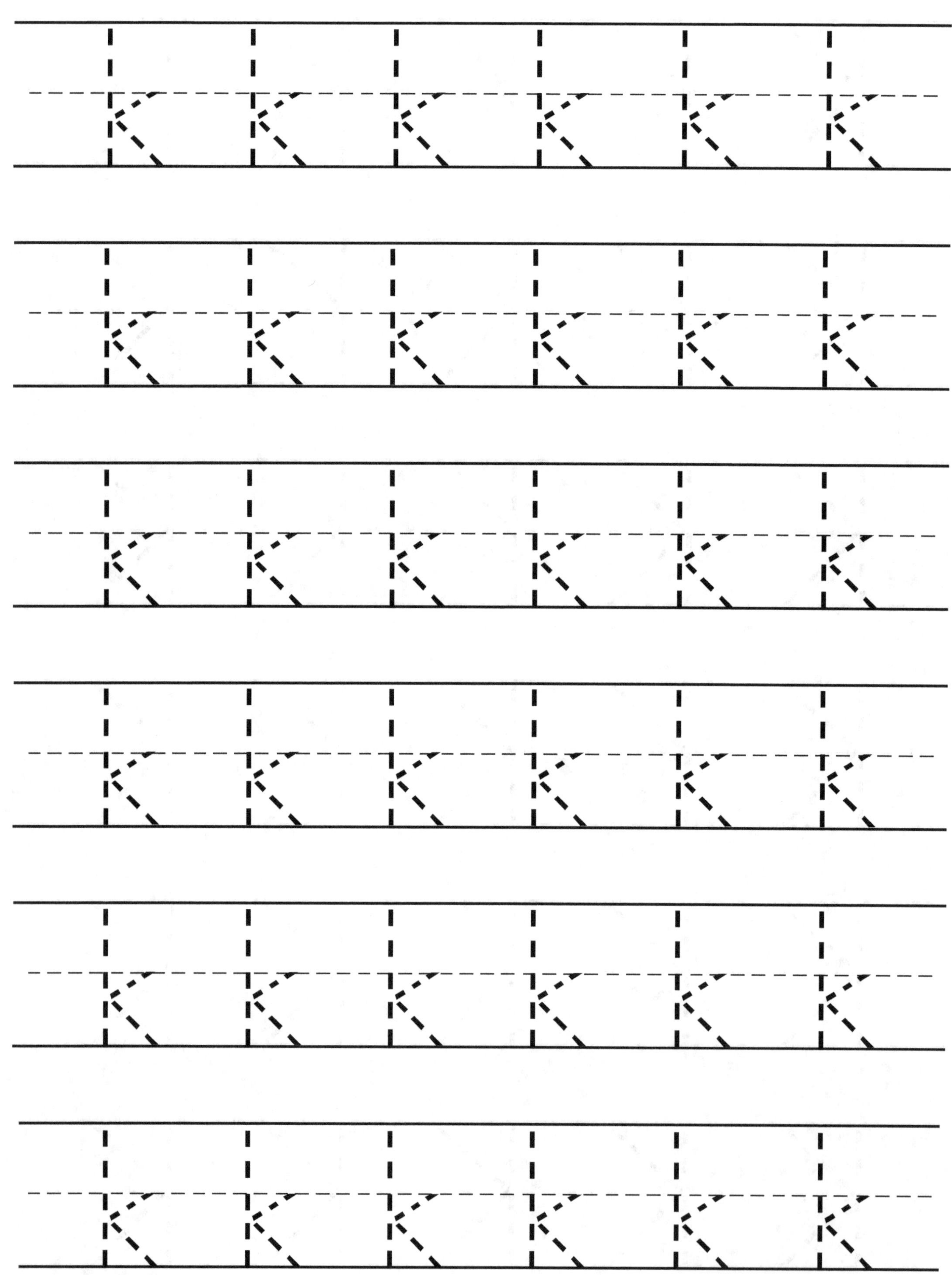

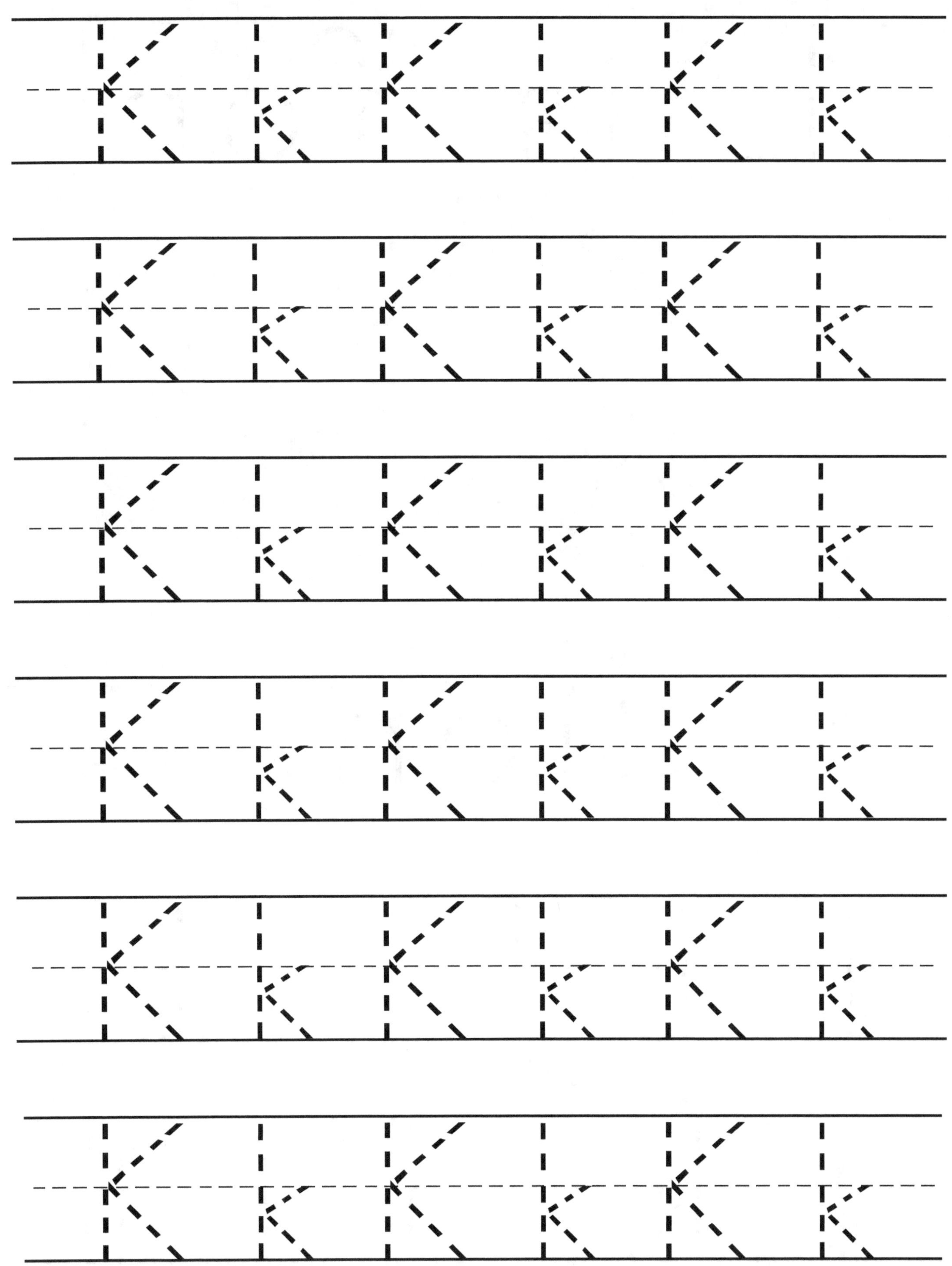

L is for

lion

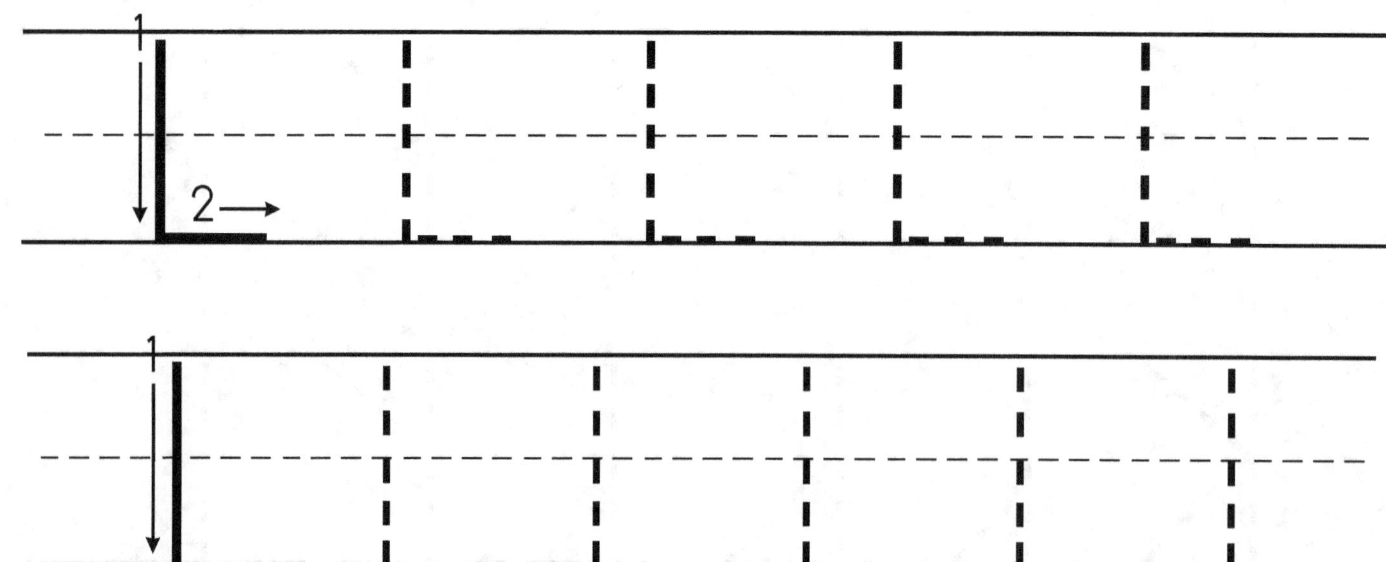

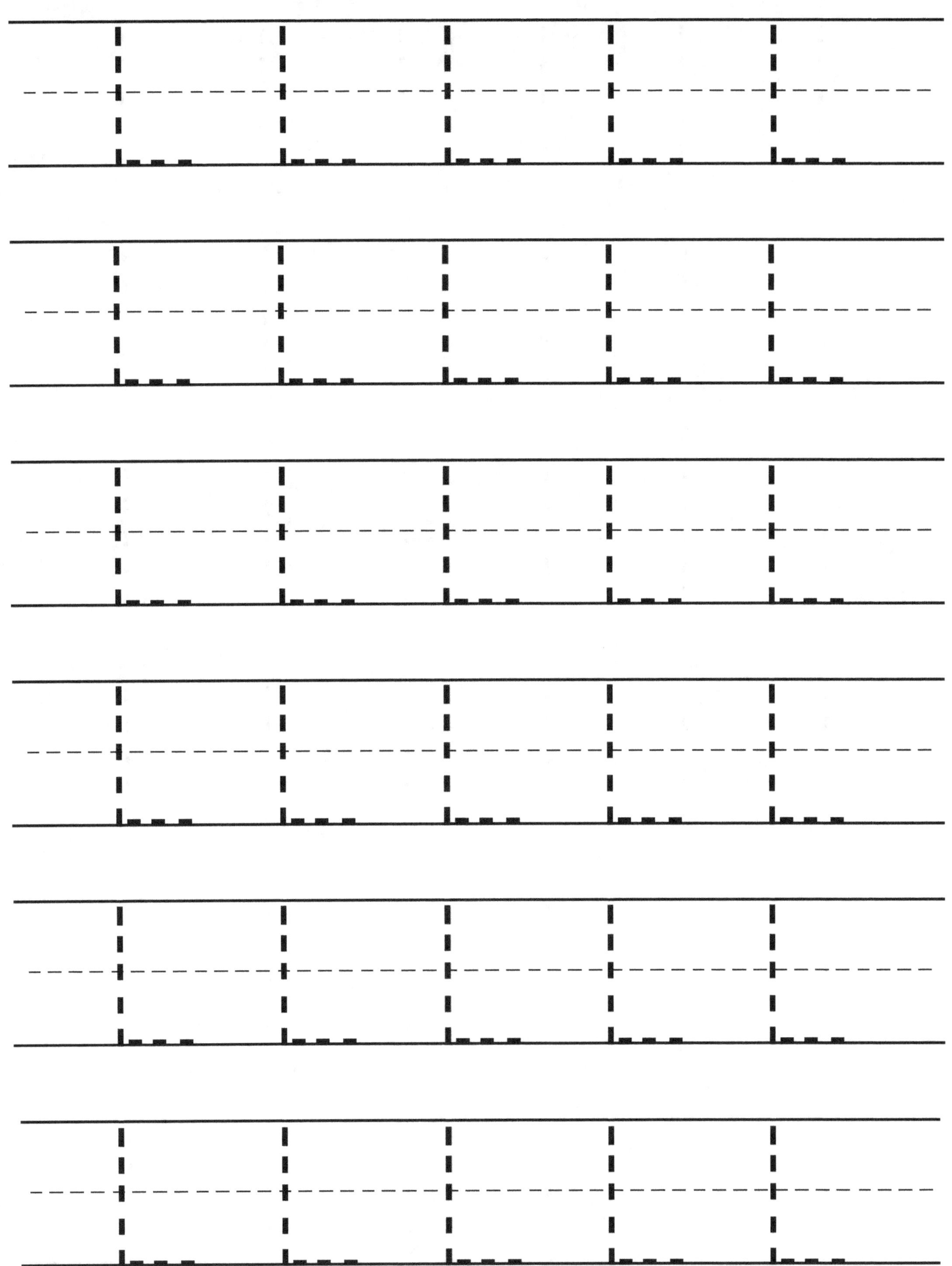

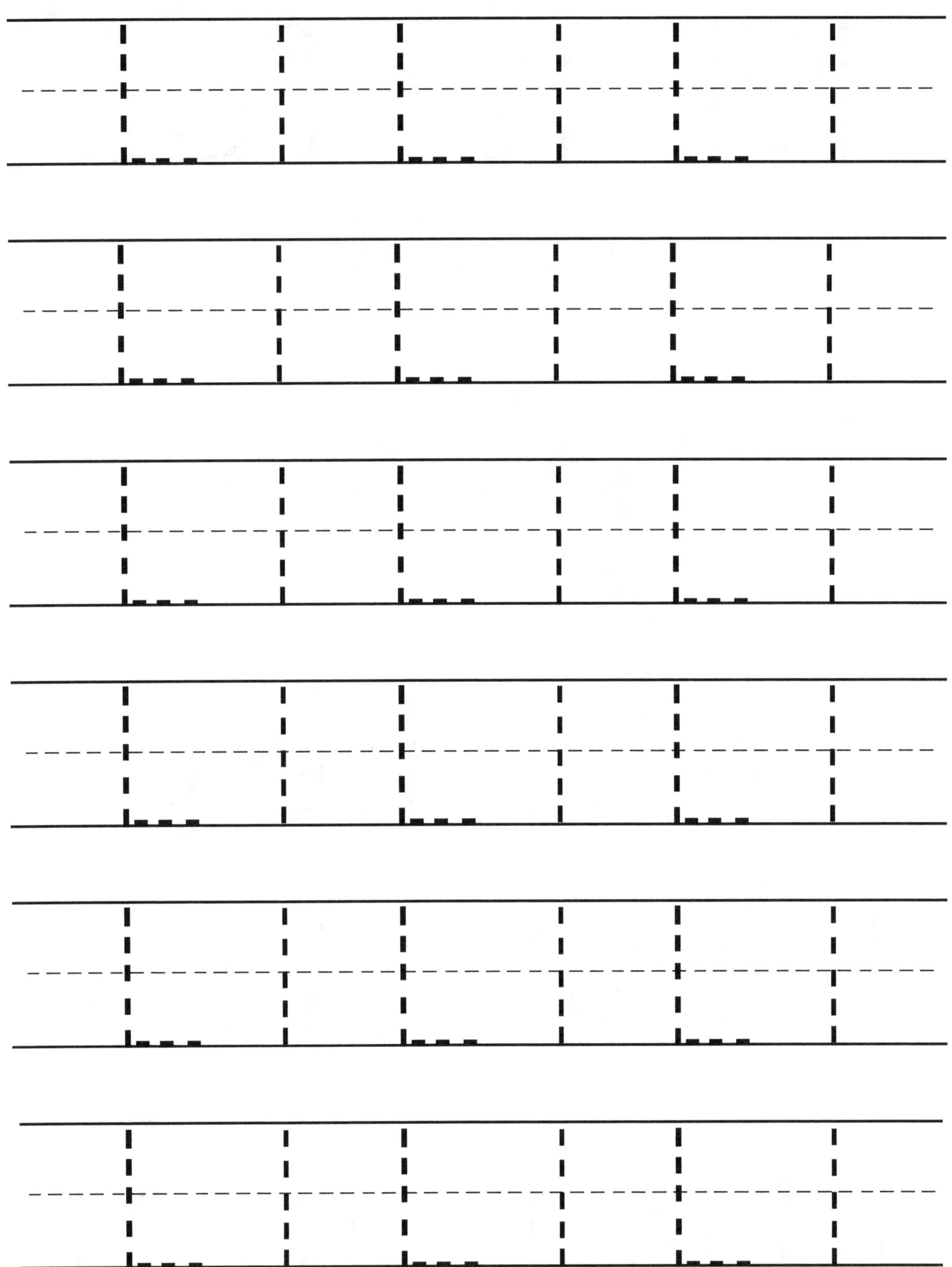

M is for

monkey

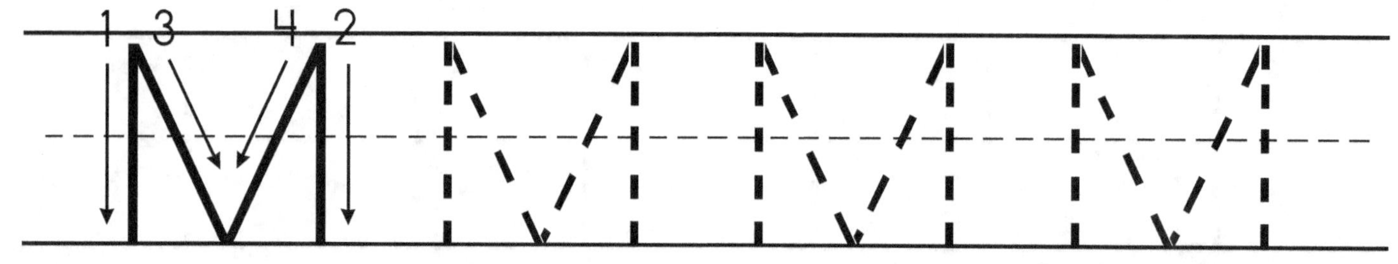

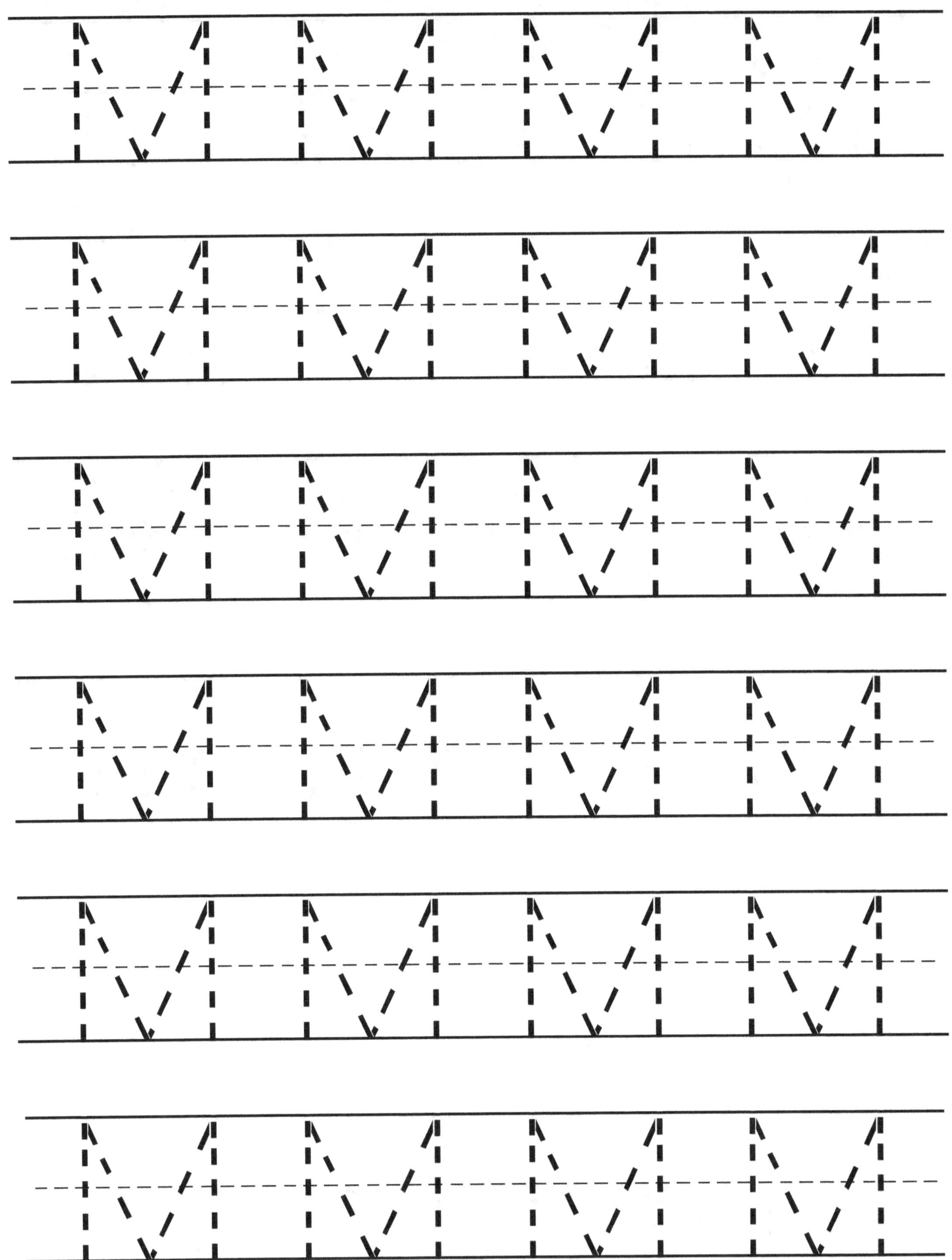

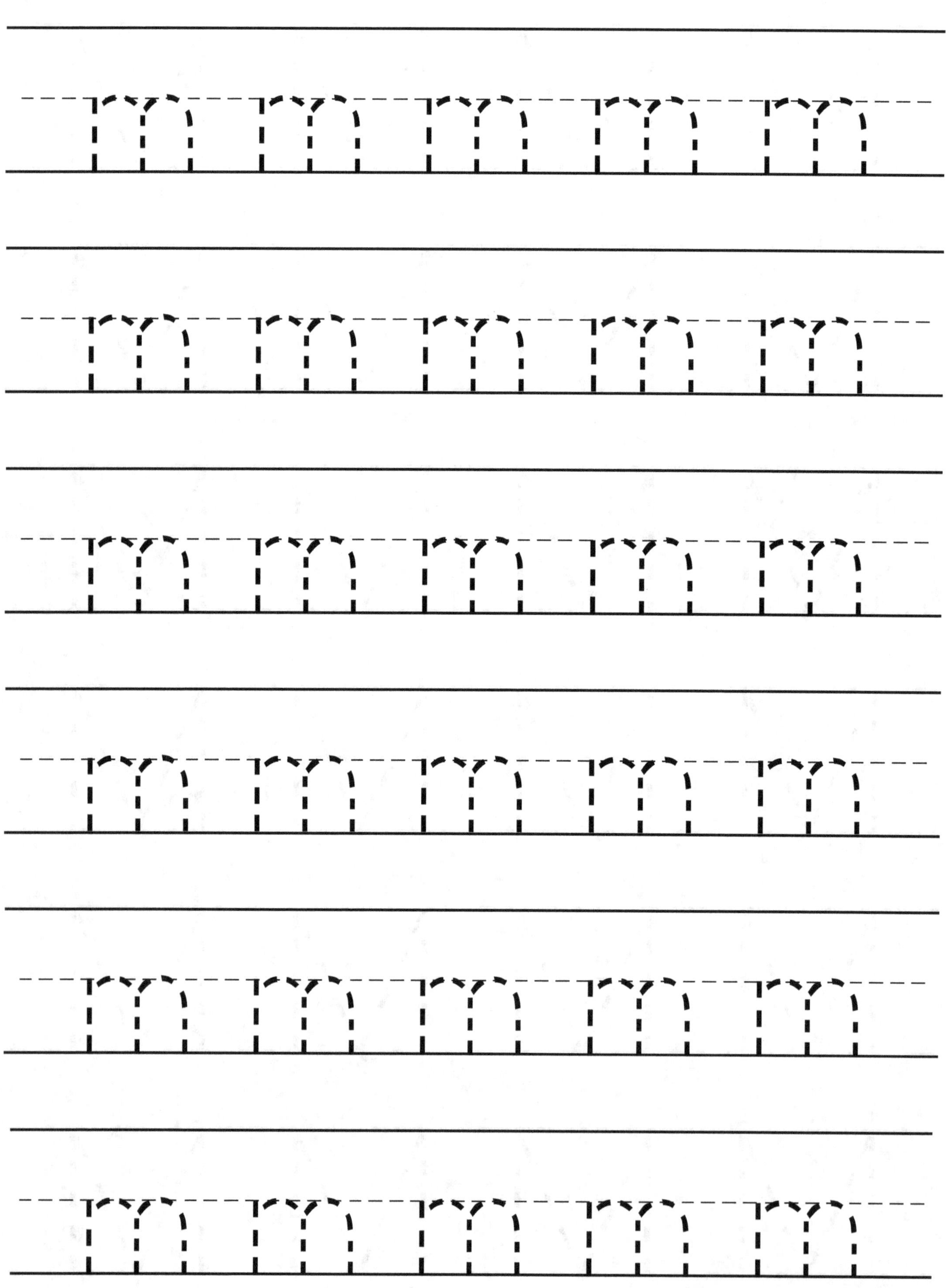

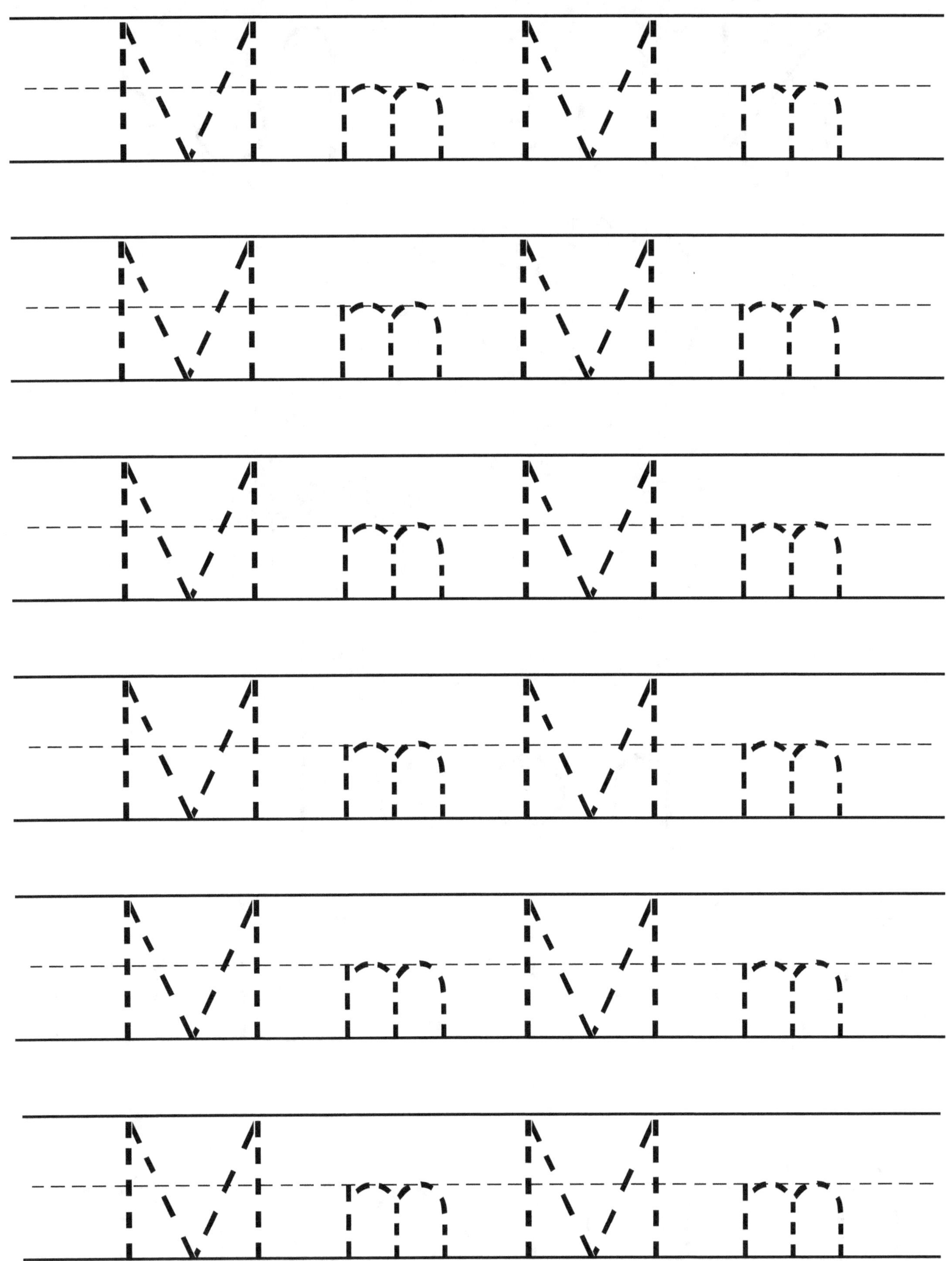

N is for

newt

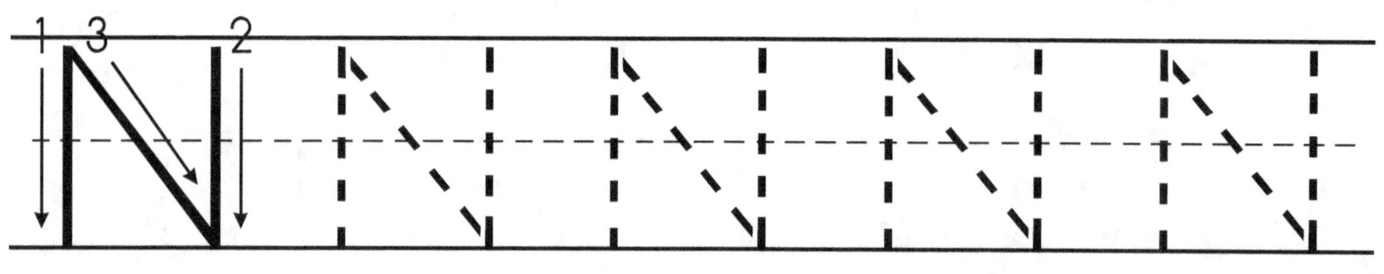

N N N N N N

N N N N N

N N N N N

N N N N N

N N N N N

N N N N N

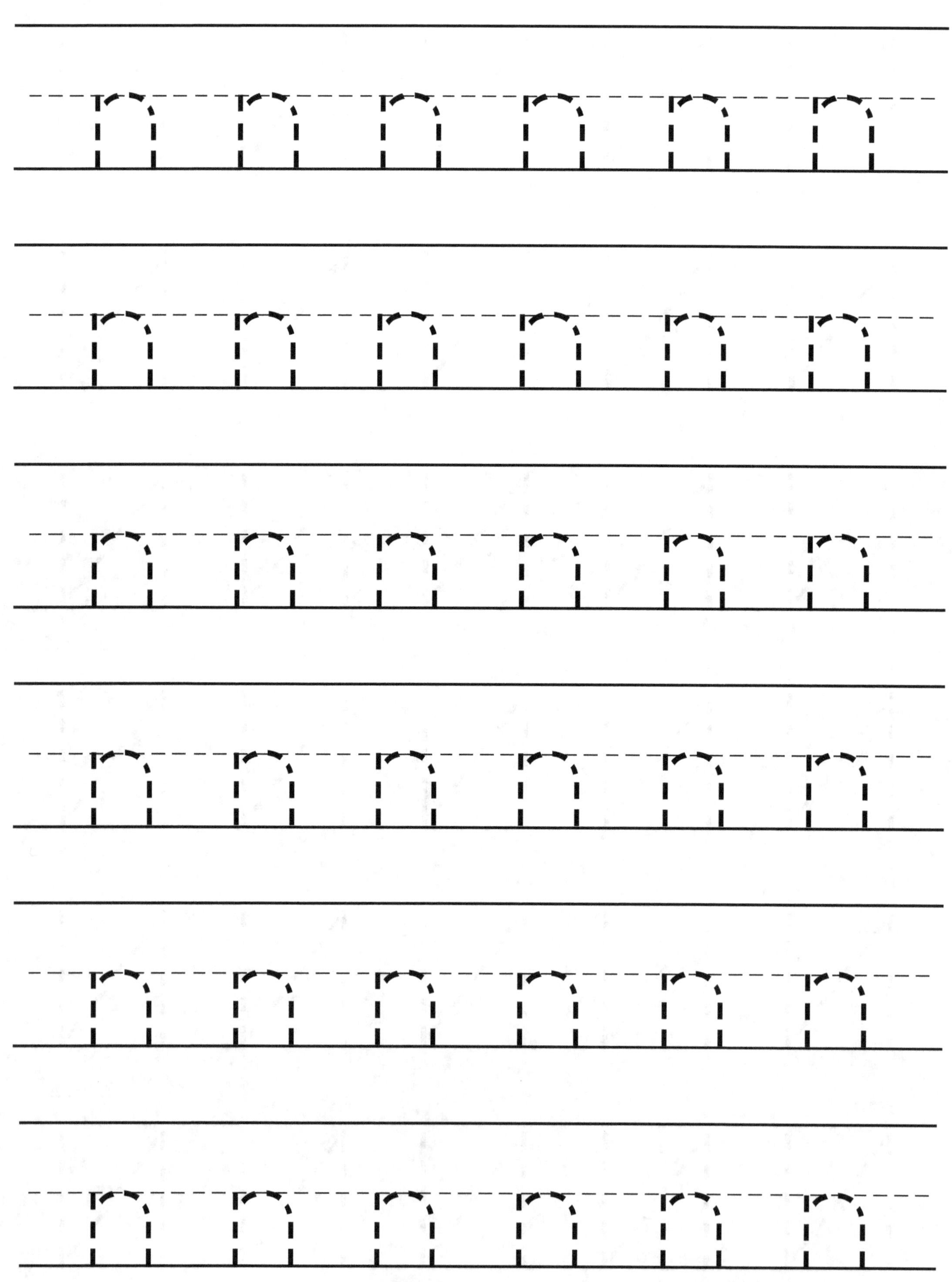

N n N n N n

N n N n N n

N n N n N n

N n N n N n

N n N n N n

N n N n N n

O is for

owl

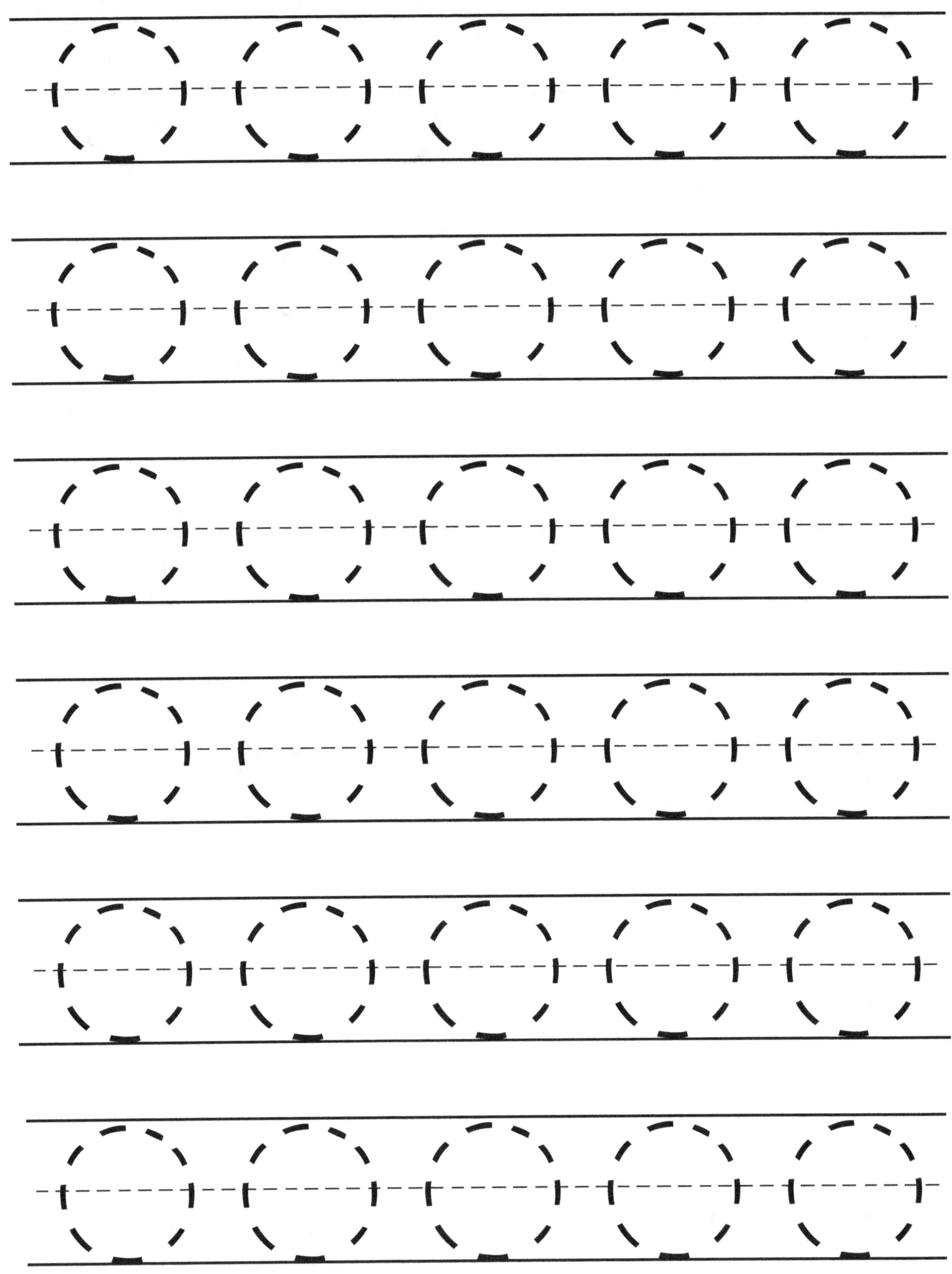

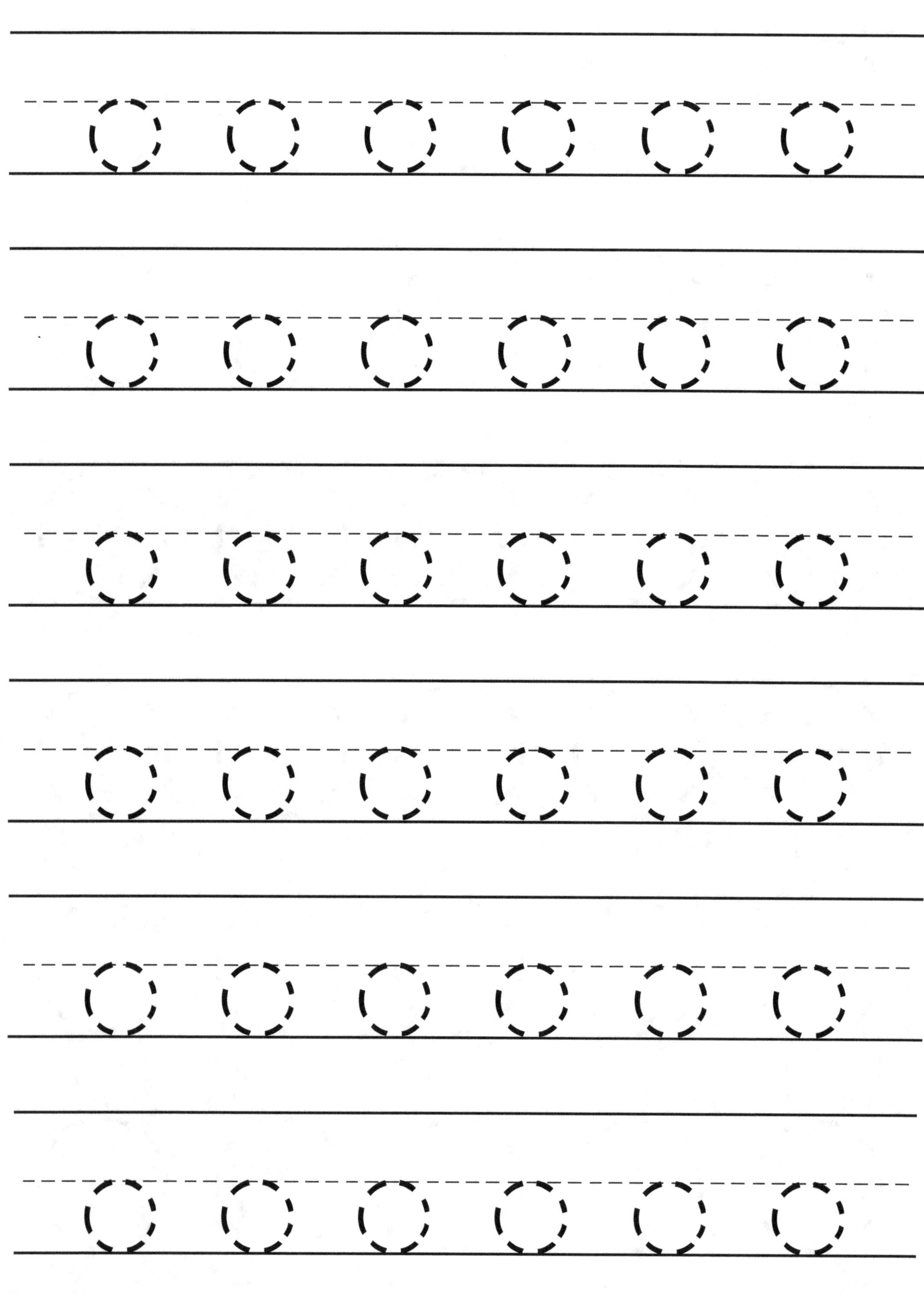

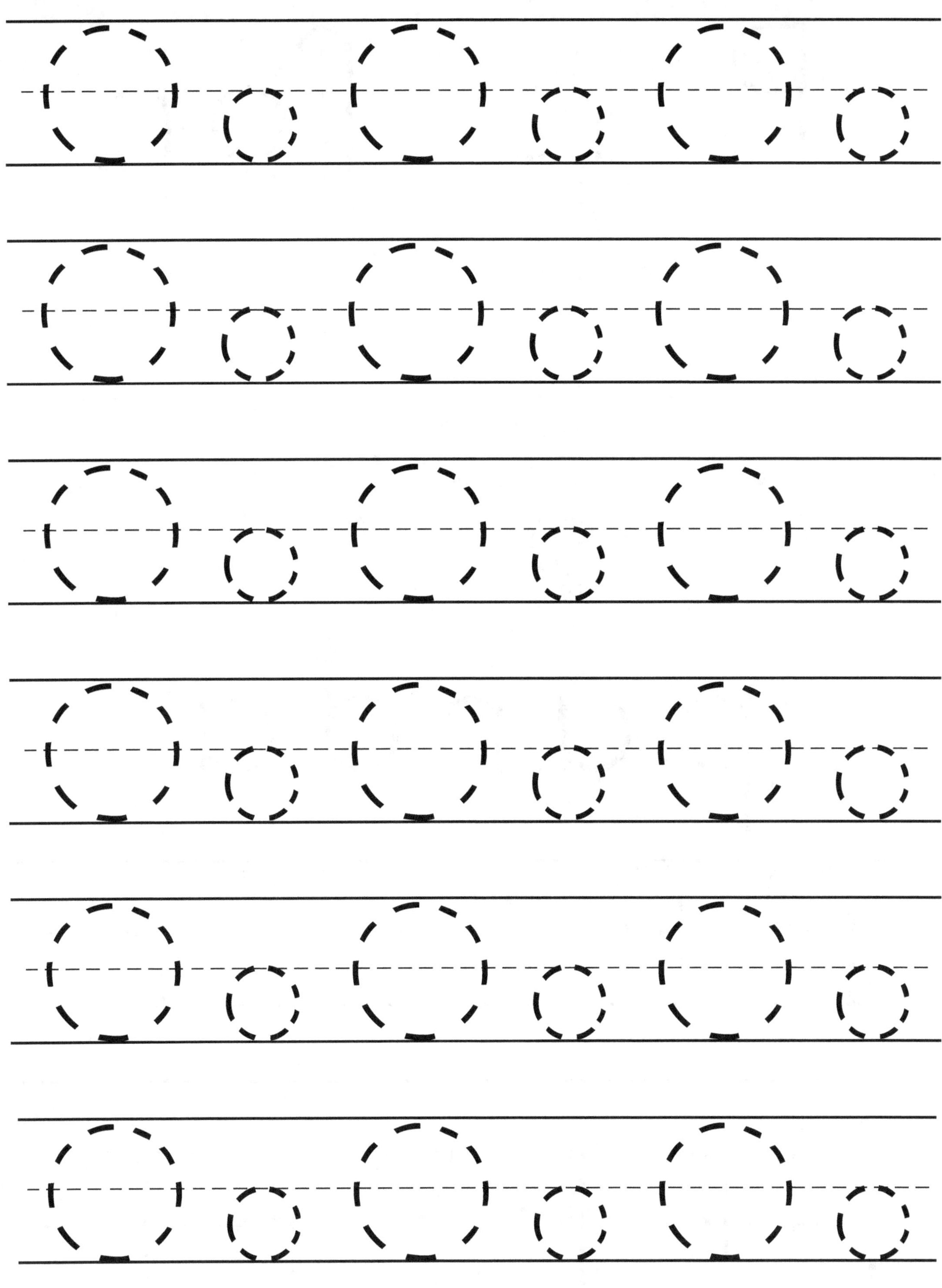

P is for

panda

P P P P P

P P P P P

P P P P P

P P P P P

P P P P P

P P P P P

p p p p p

p p p p p

p p p p p

p p p p p

p p p p p

p p p p p

Q is for
quail

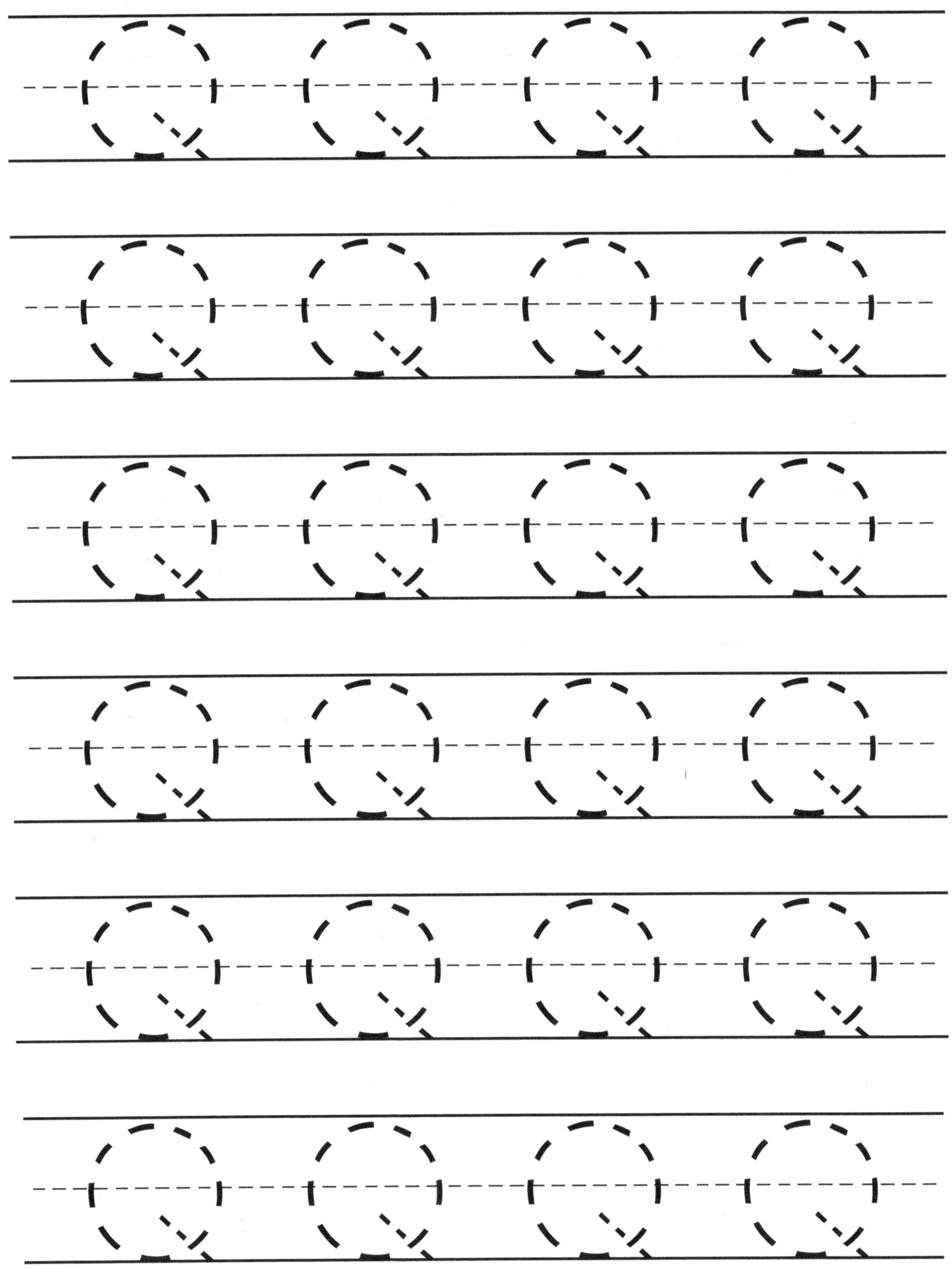

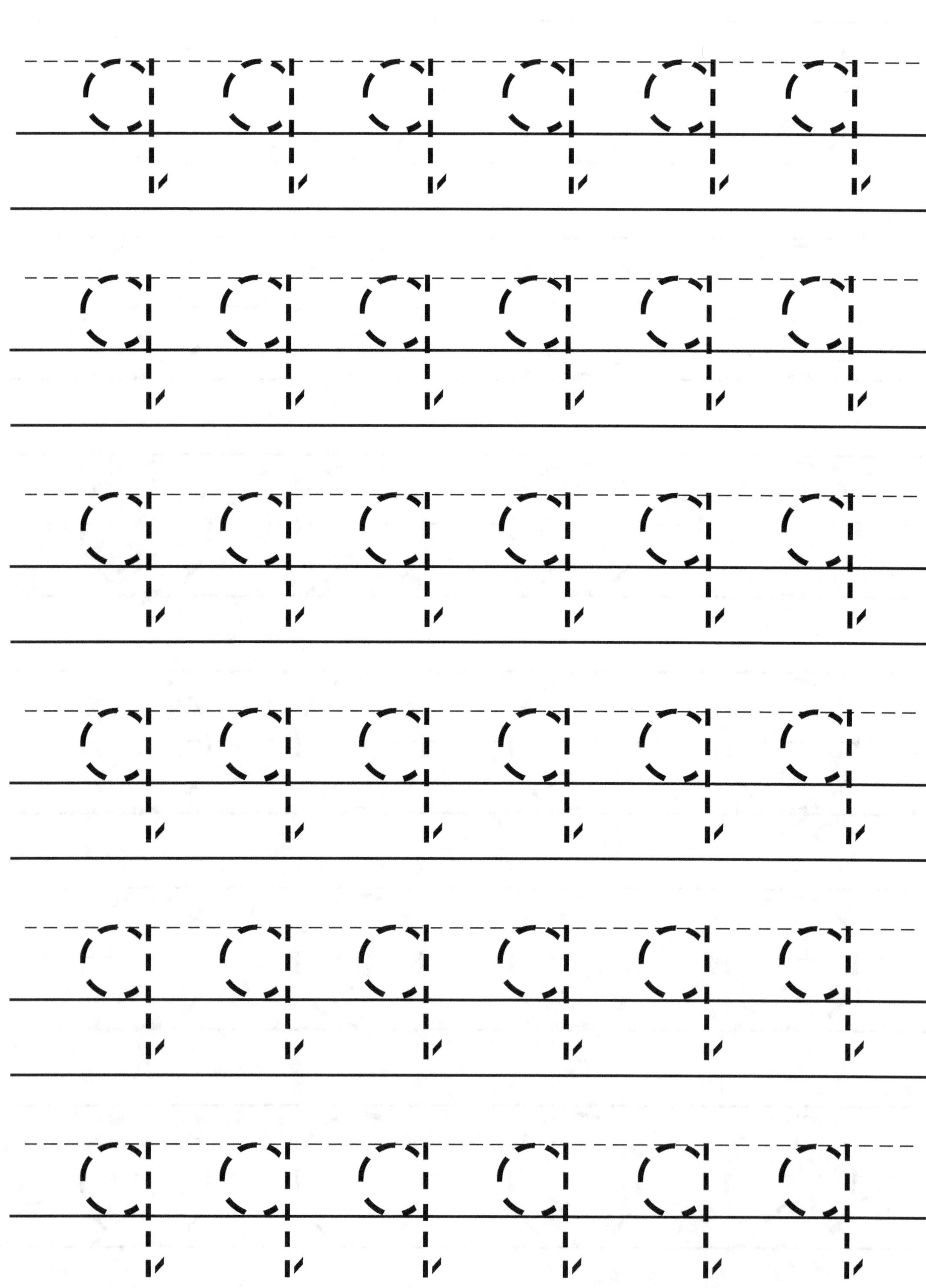

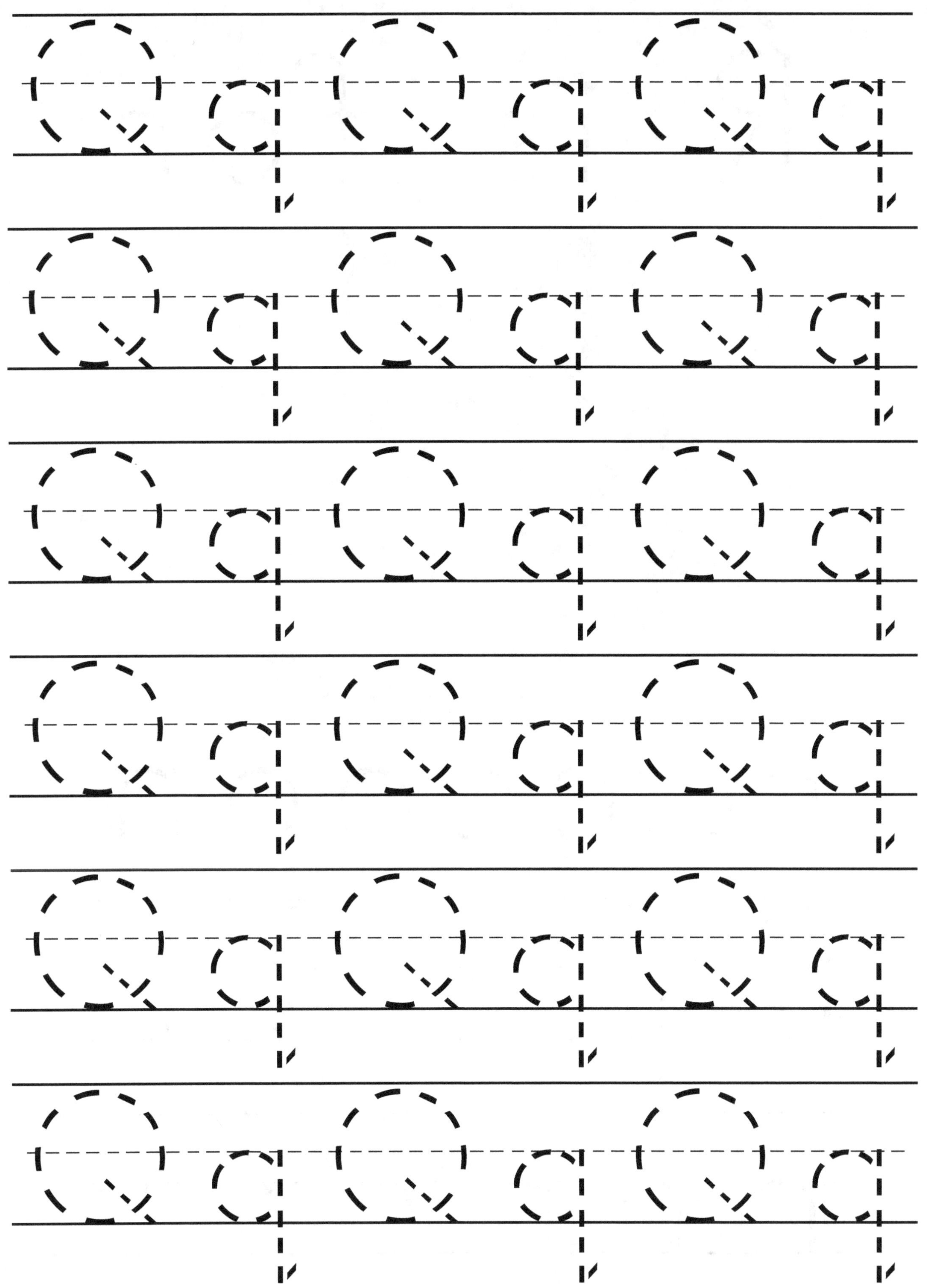

R is for

raccoon

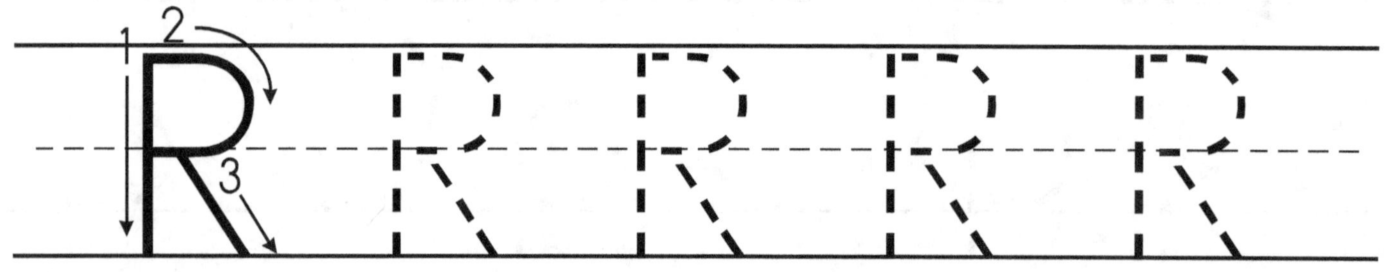

R R R R R

R R R R R

R R R R R

R R R R R

R R R R R

R R R R R

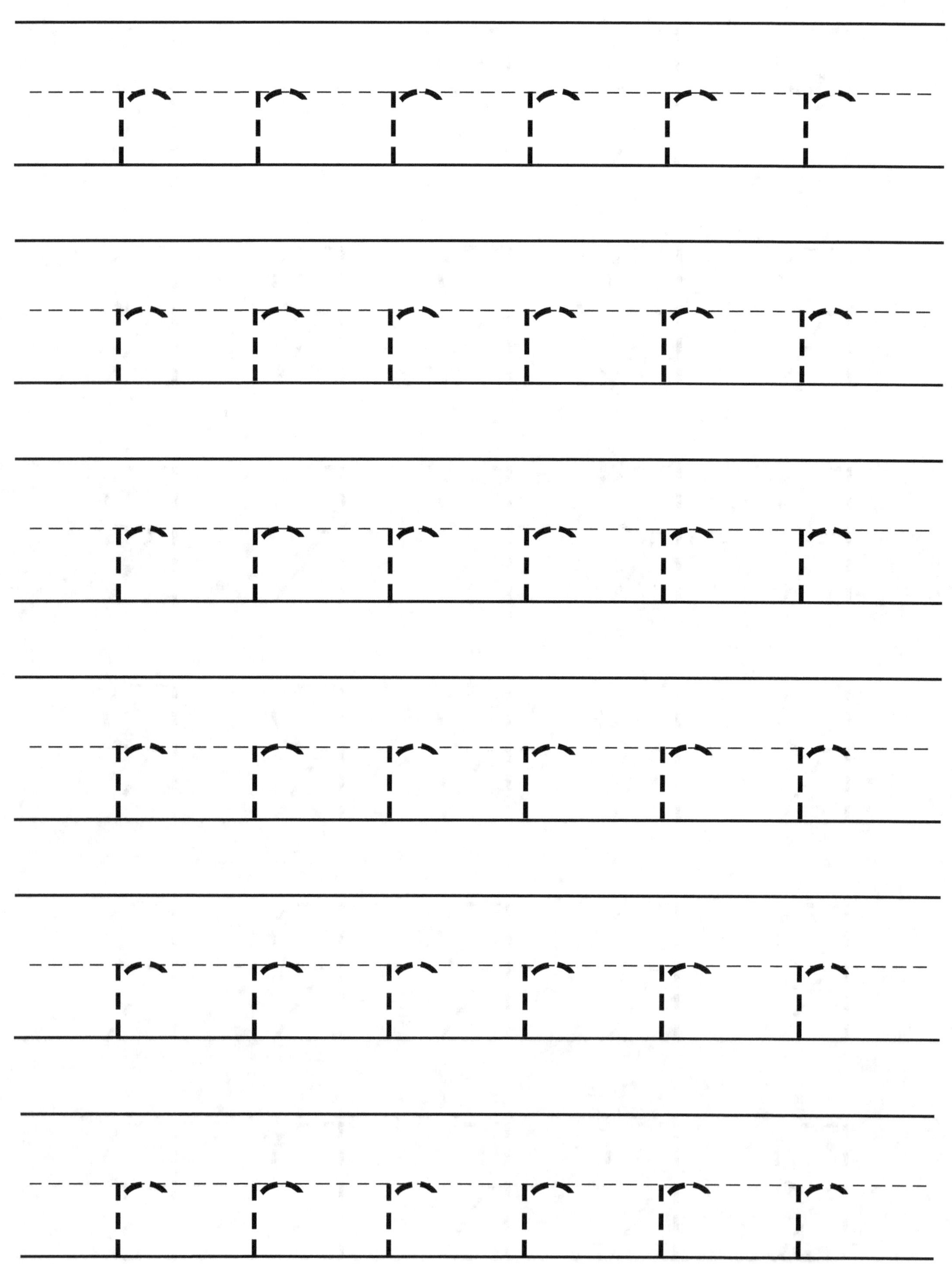

R r   R r   R r

R r   R r   R r

R r   R r   R r

R r   R r   R r

R r   R r   R r

R r   R r   R r

S is for

squirrel

S S S S S

S s s s s s s

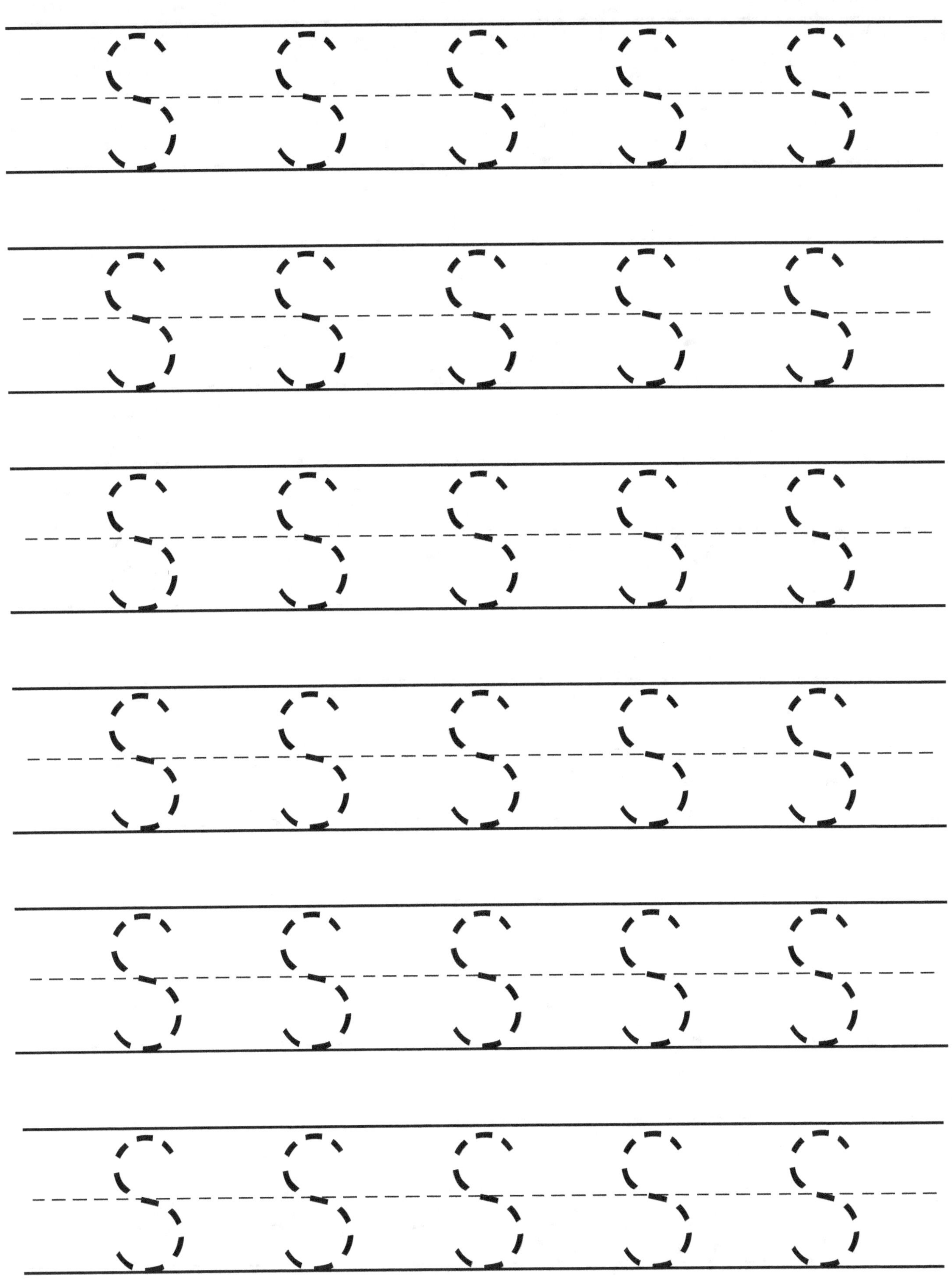

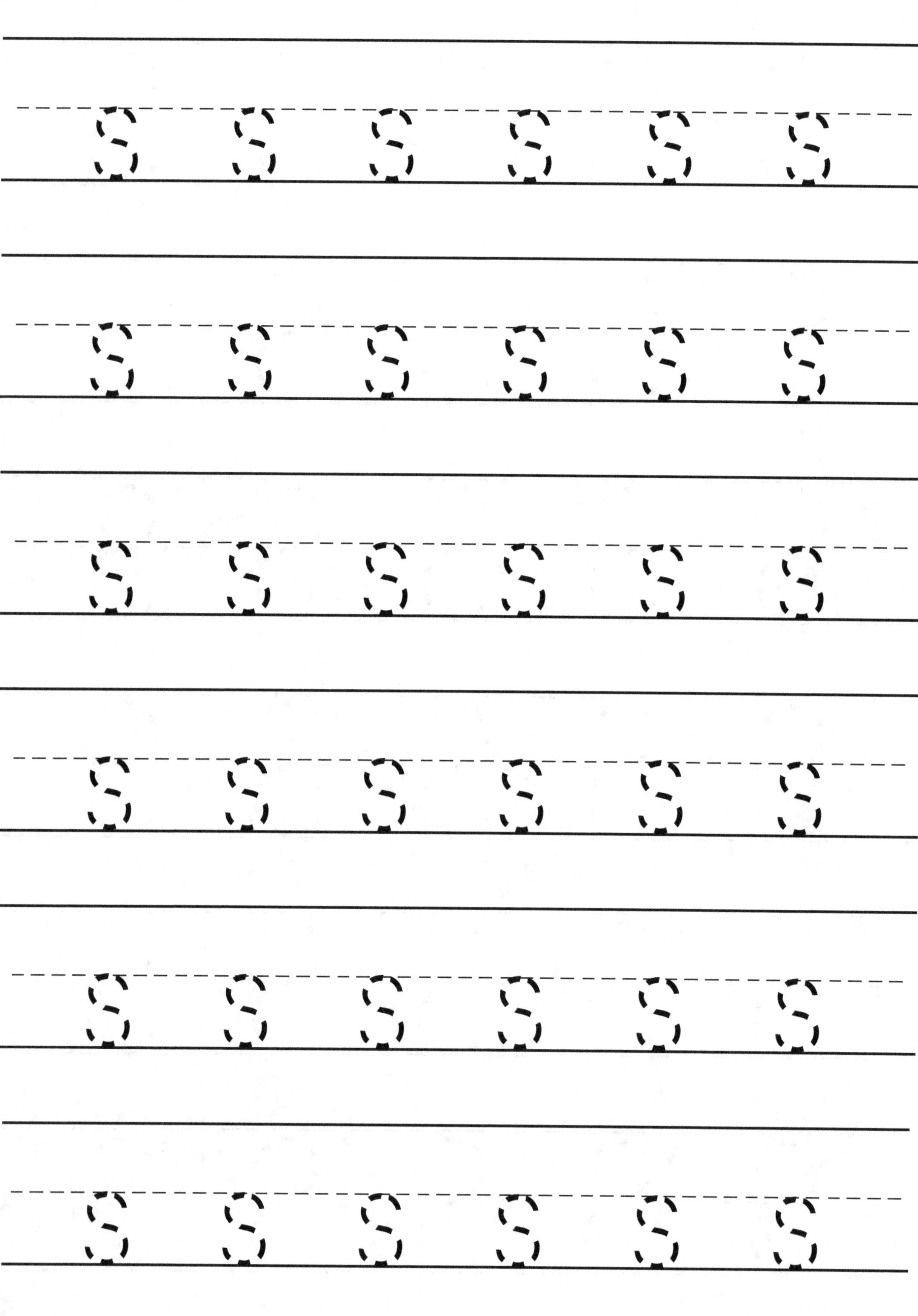

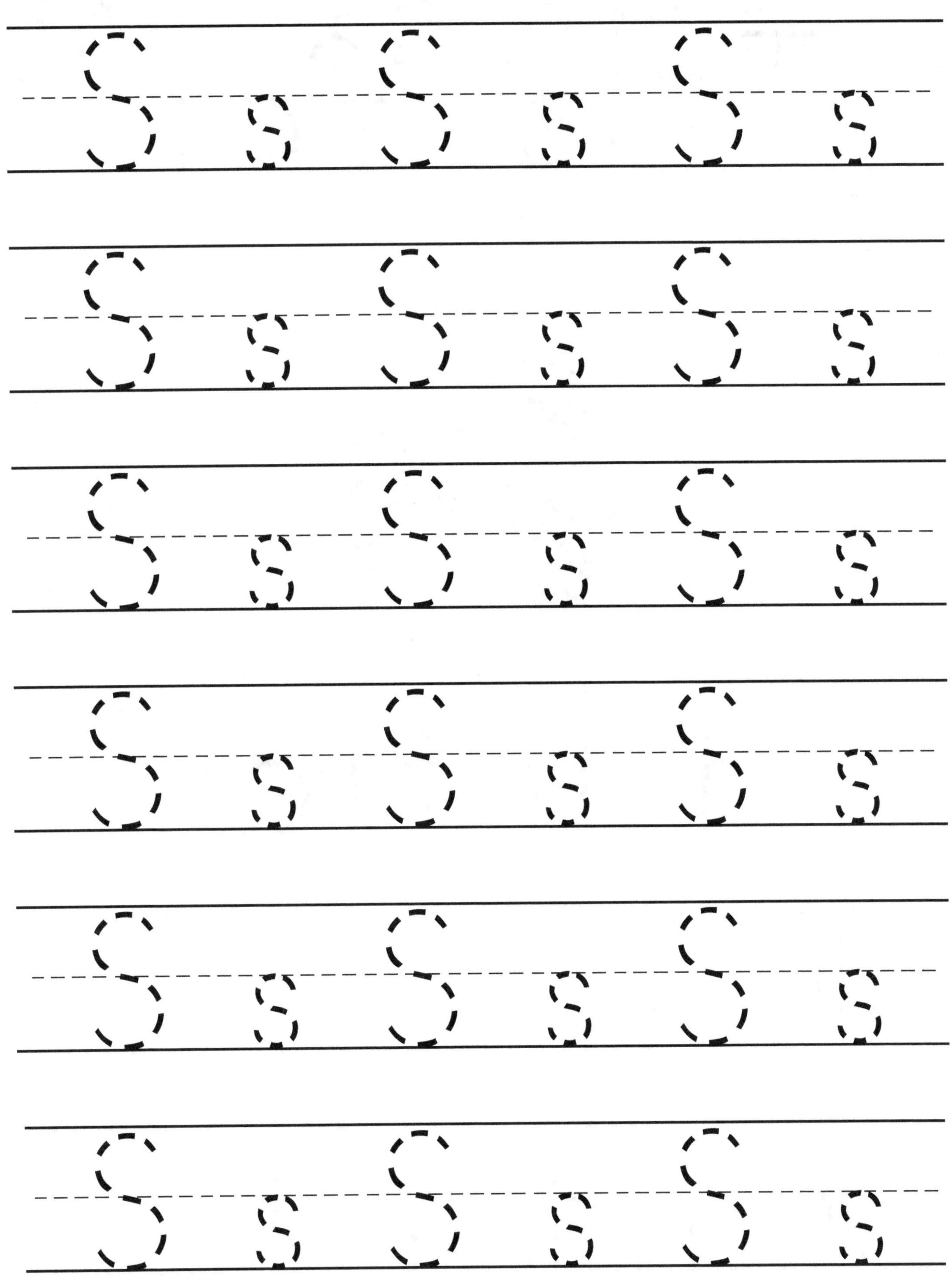

T is for

turtle

T T T T T

T T T T T

T T T T T

T T T T T

T T T T T

T T T T T

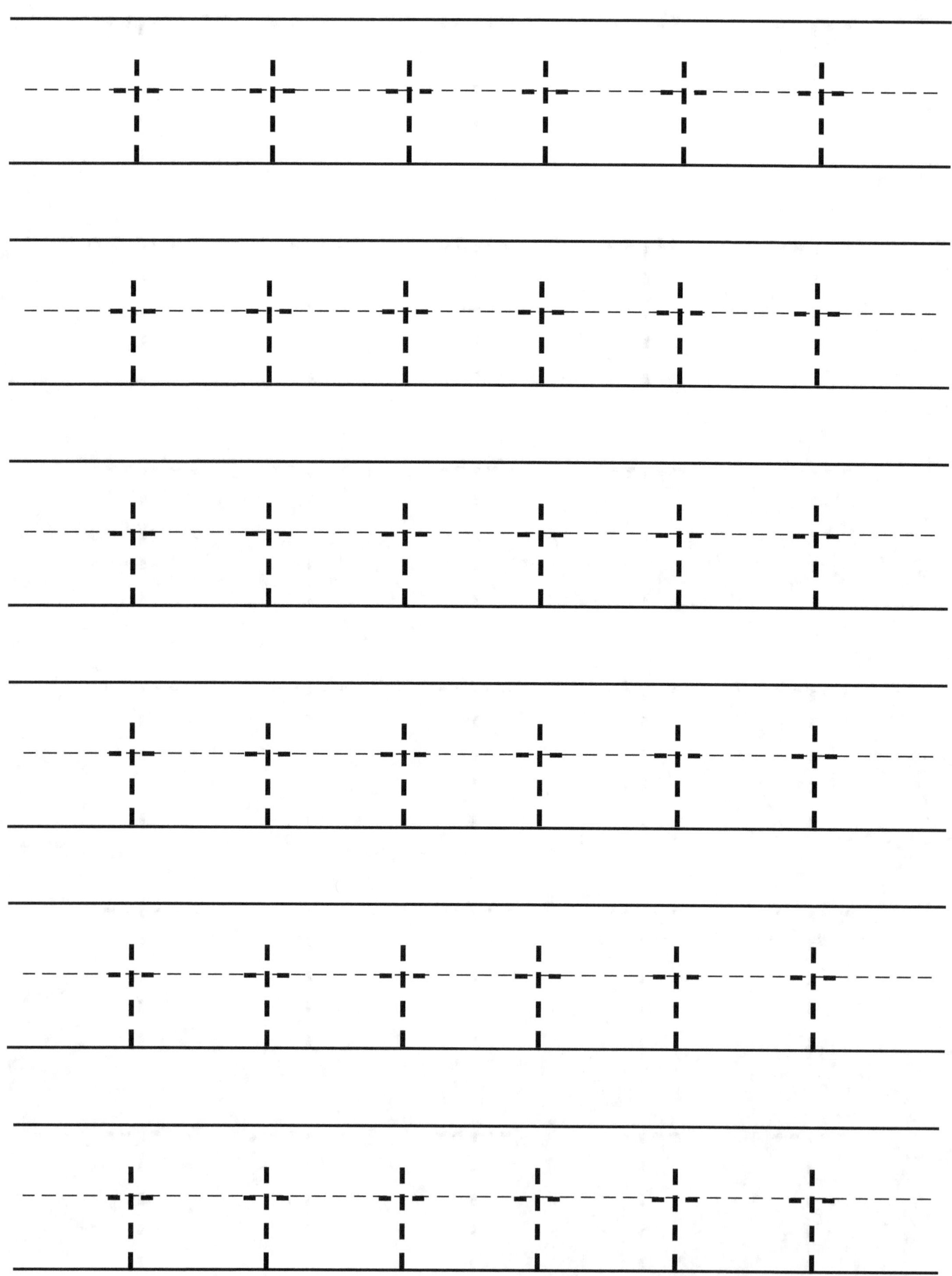

U is for

unicorn

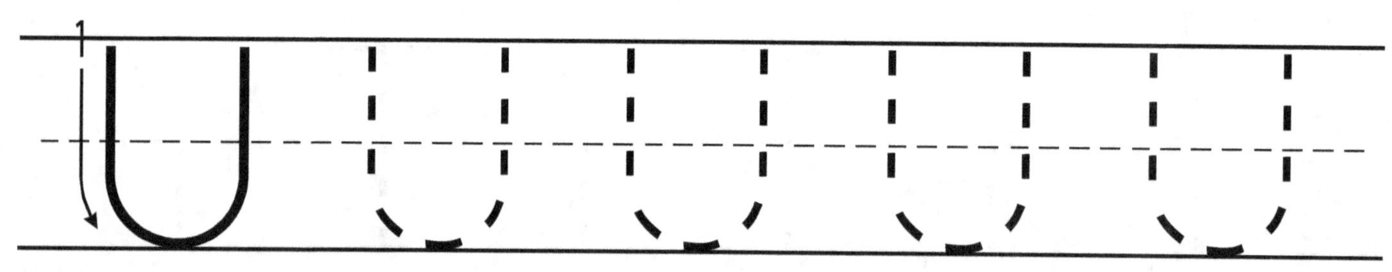

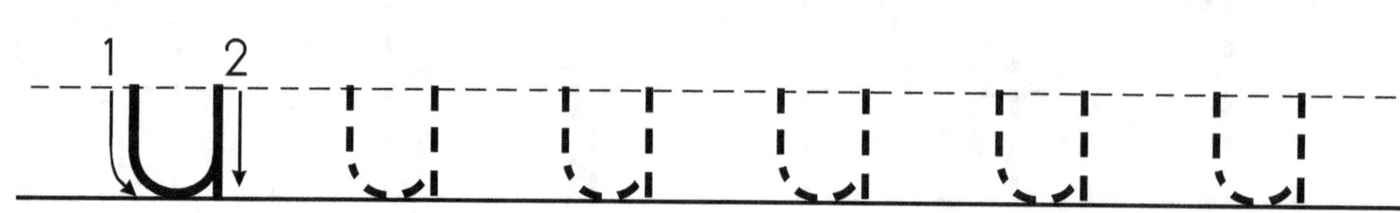

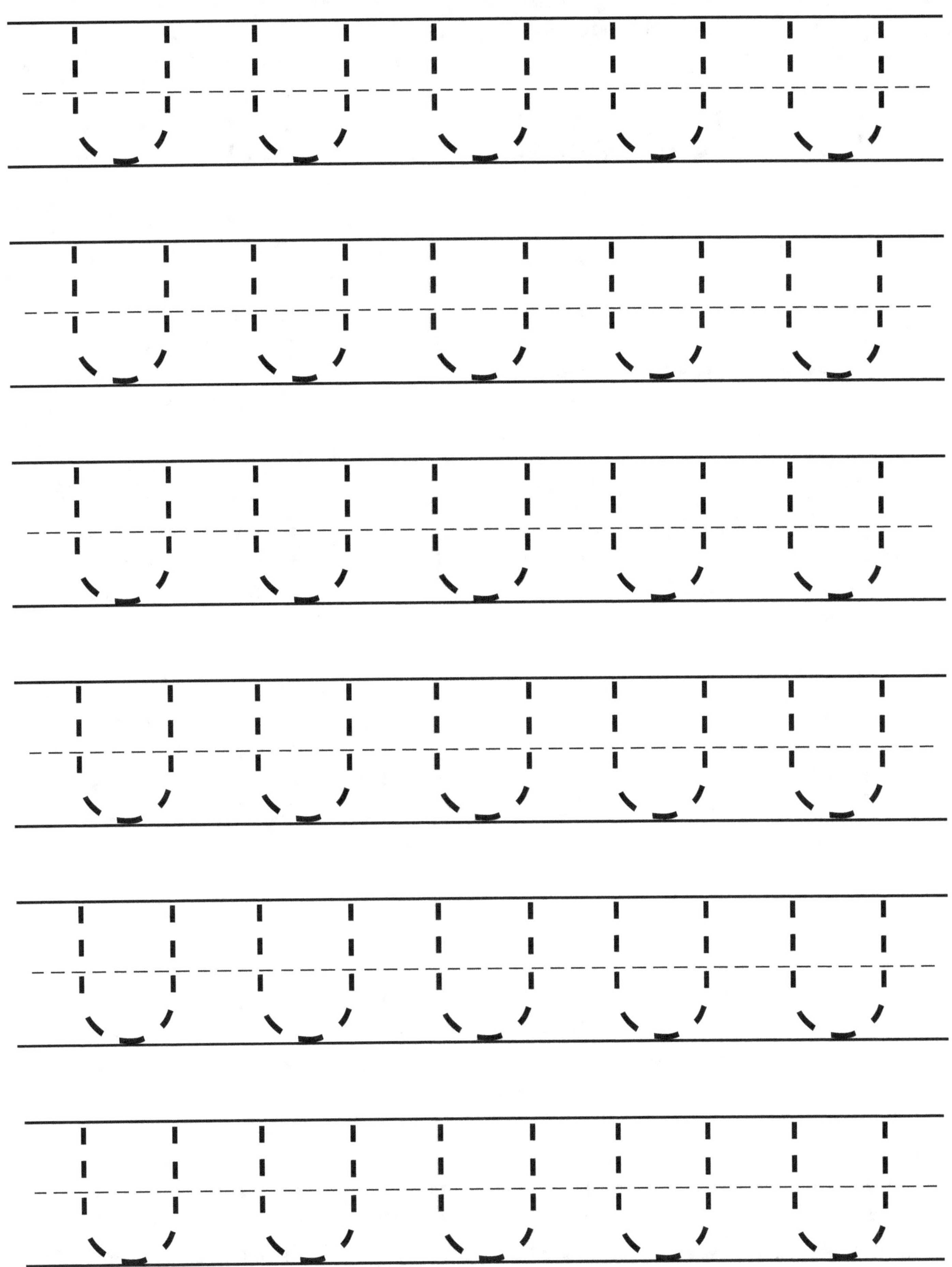

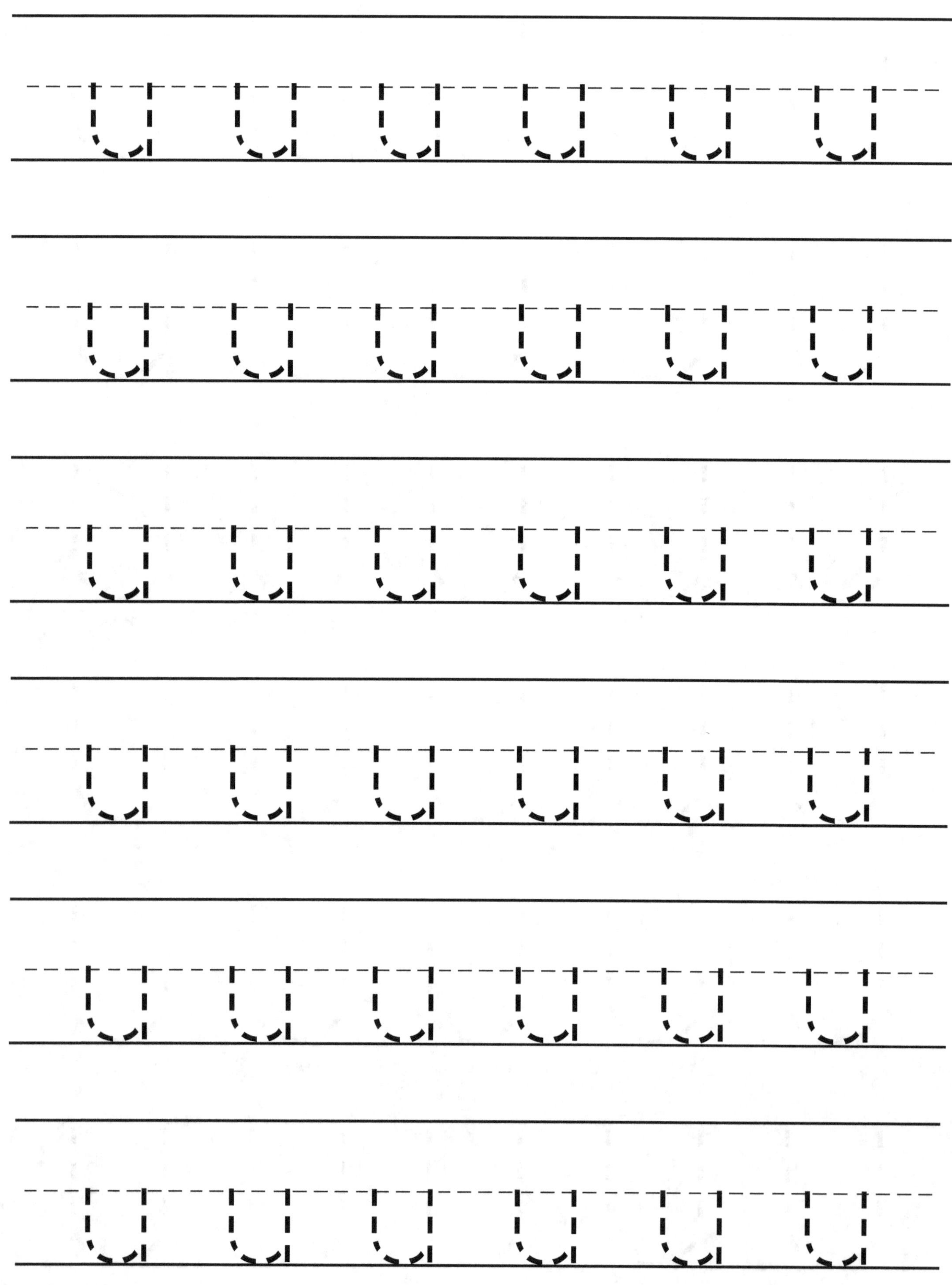

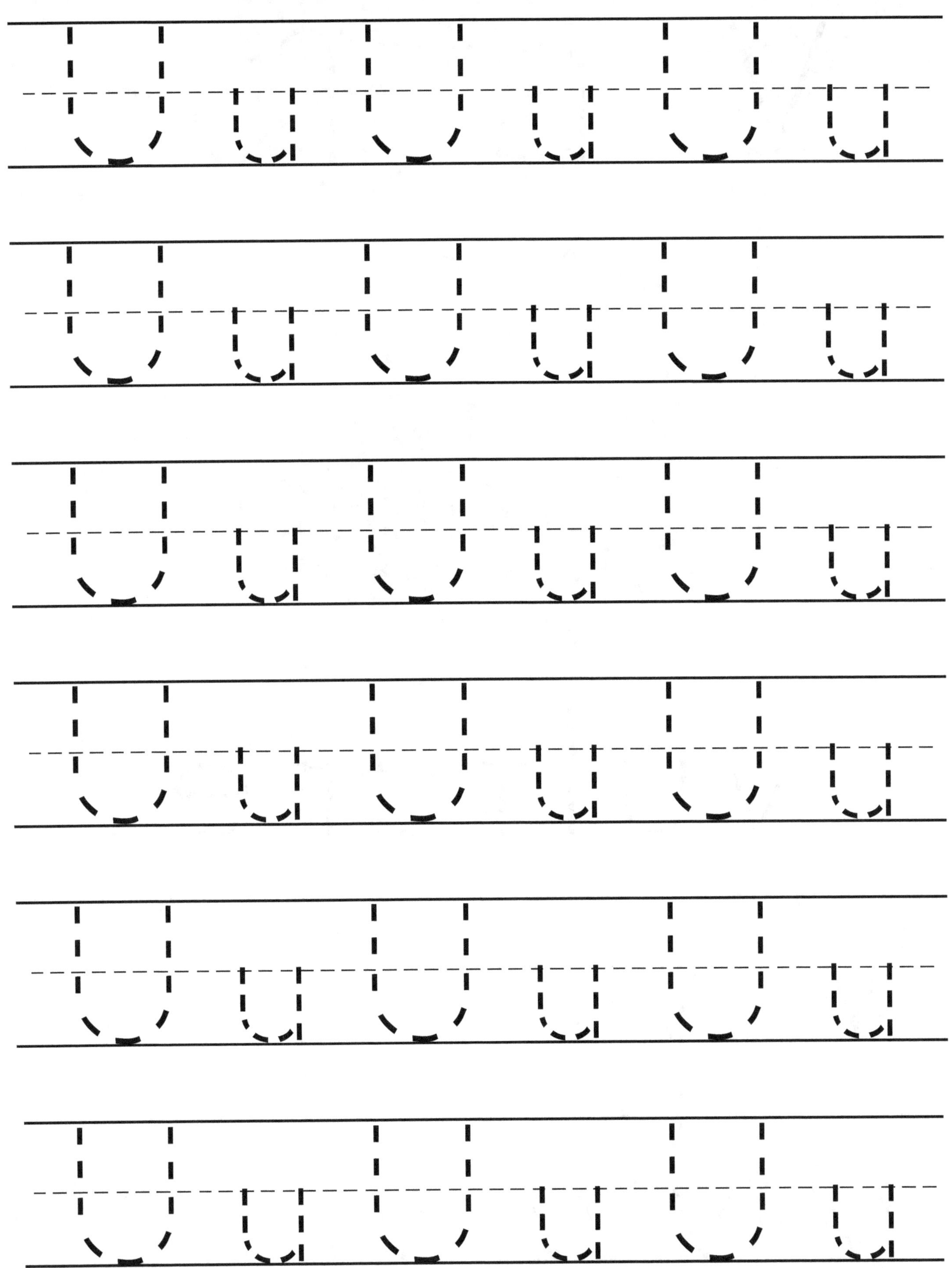

V is for

vulture

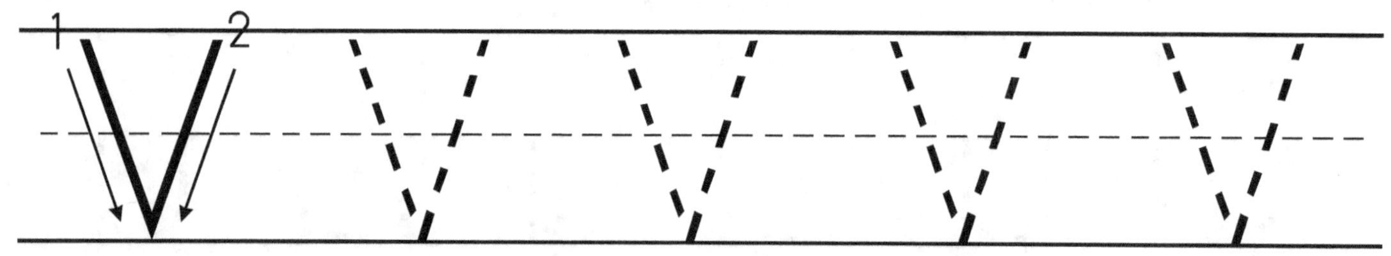

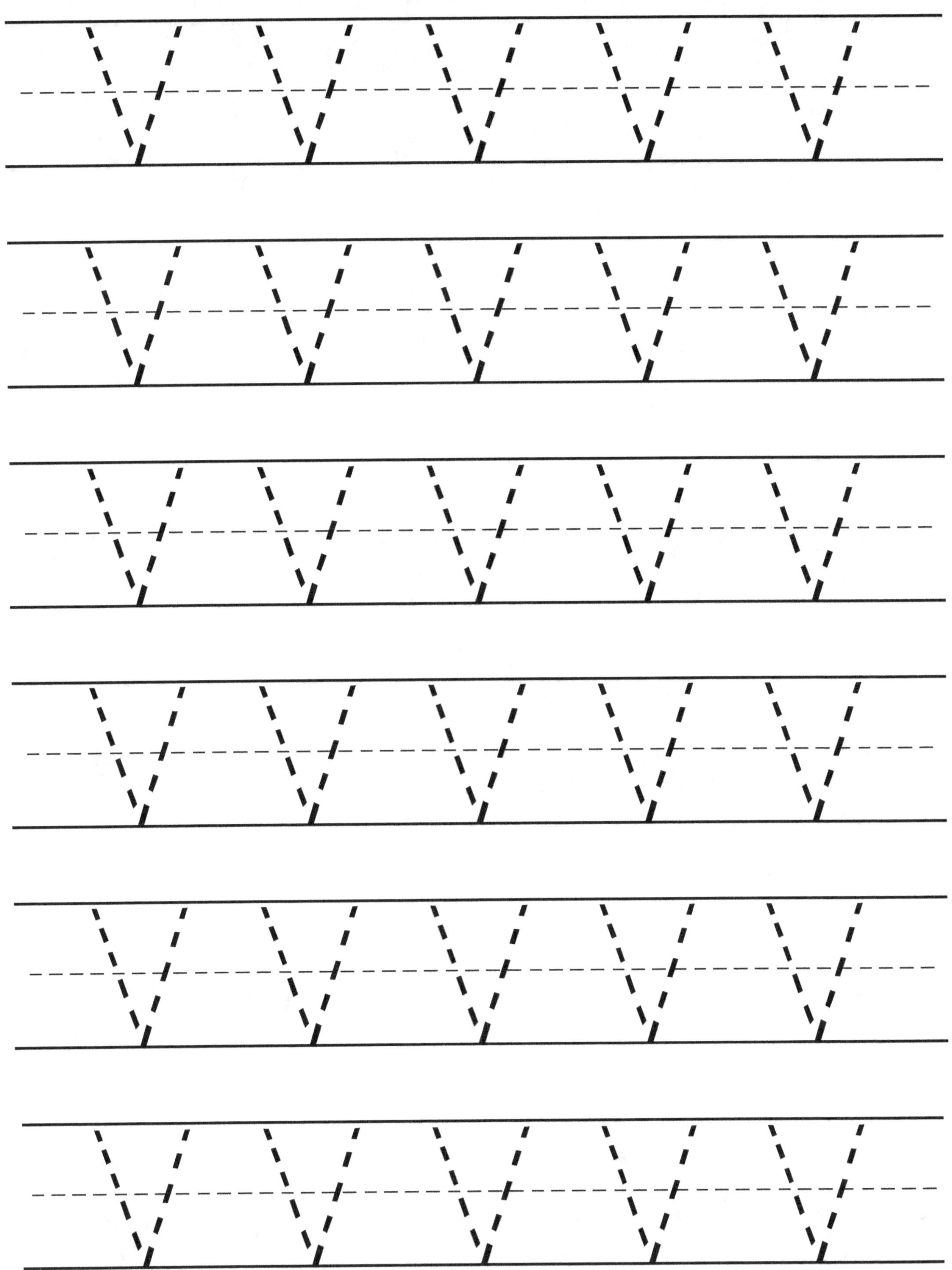

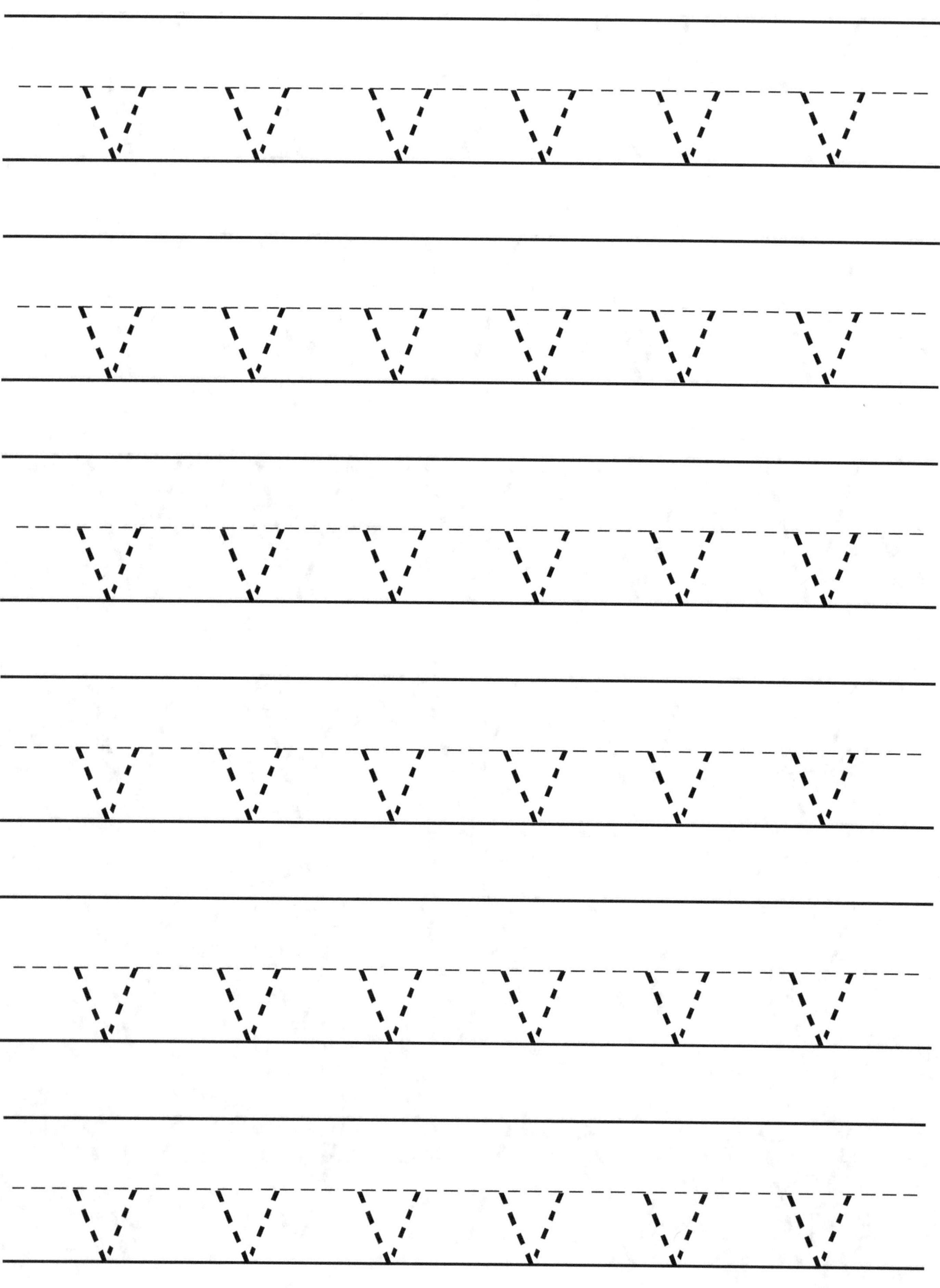

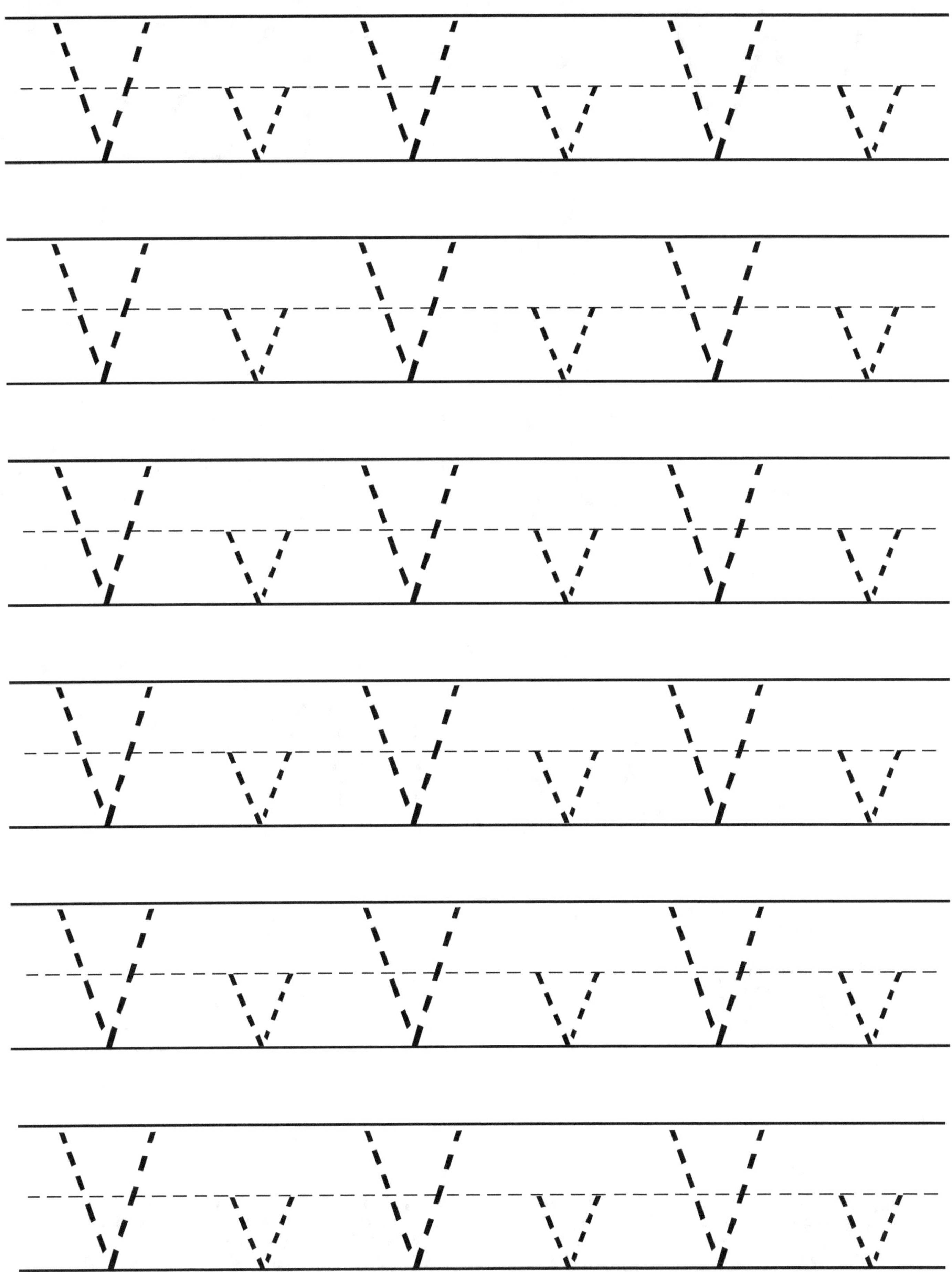

W is for

wolf

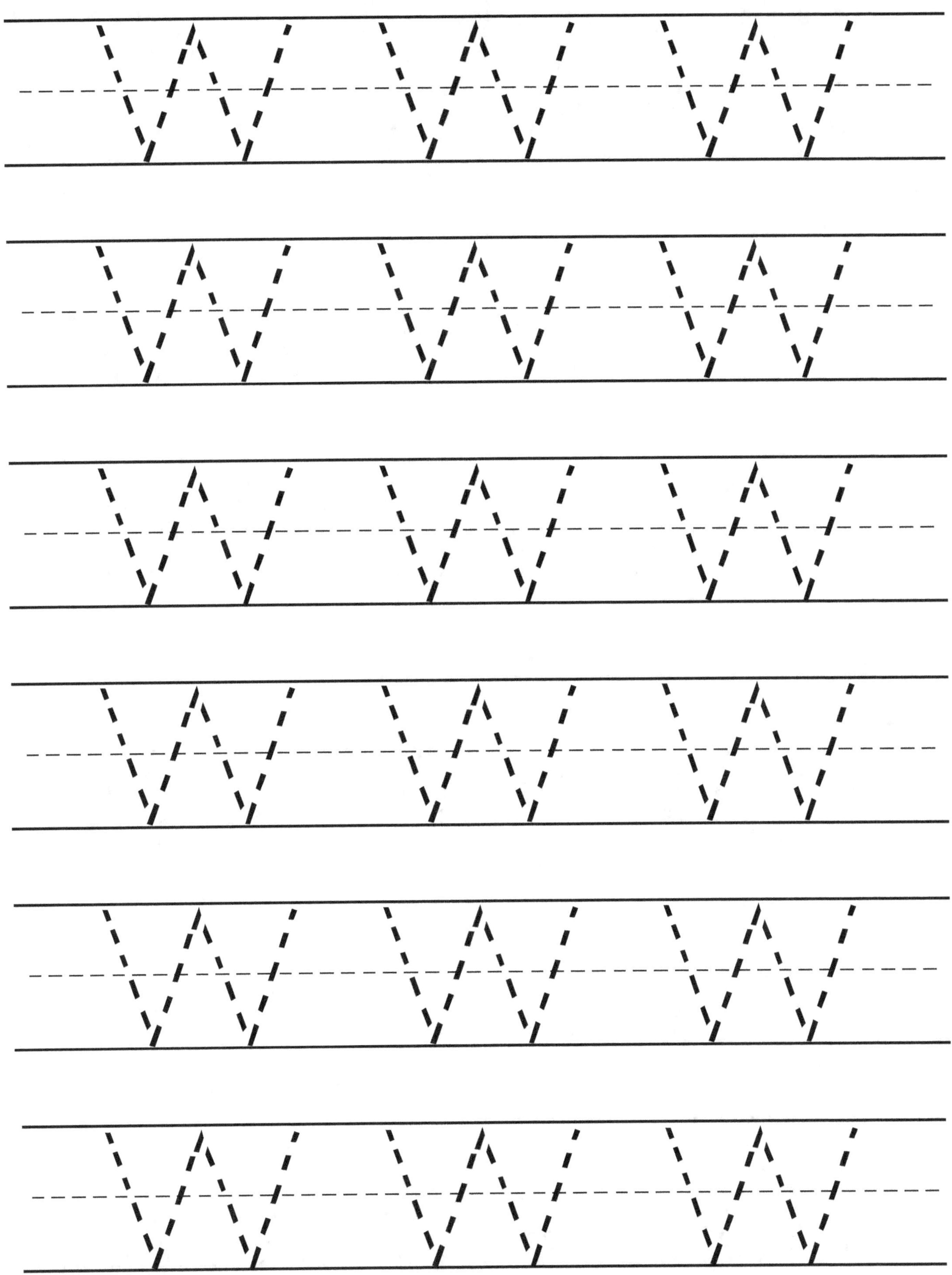

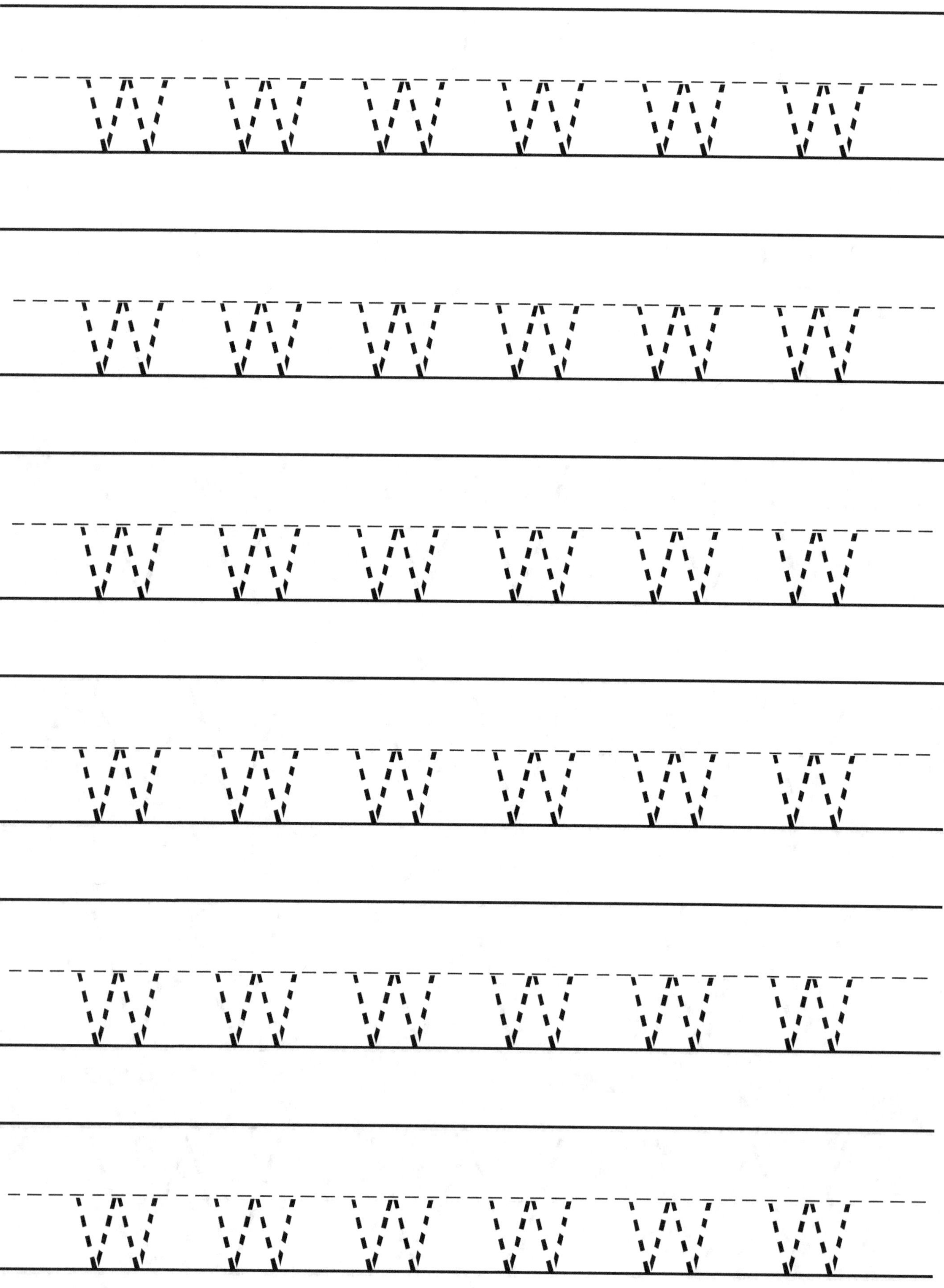

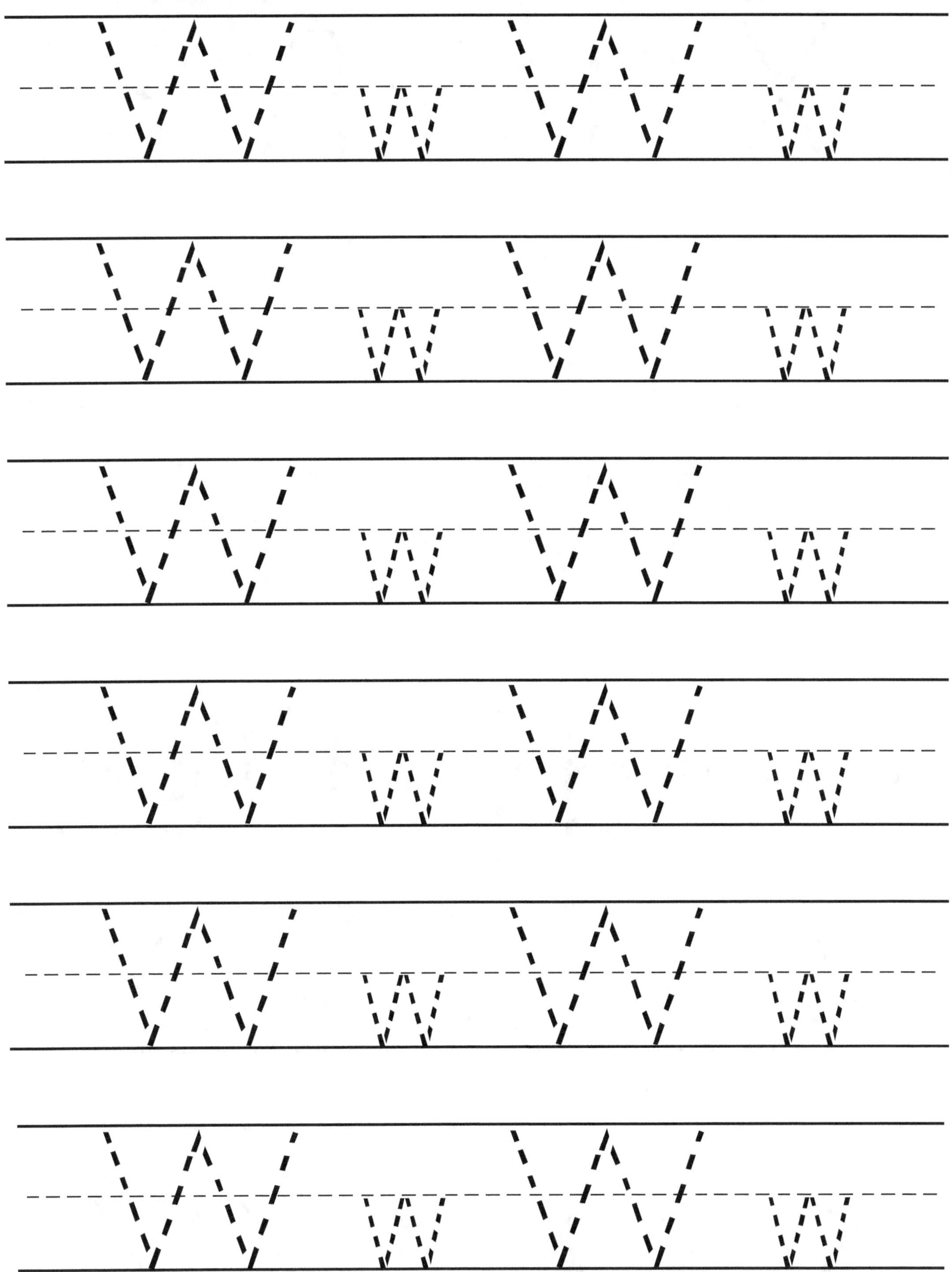

X is for

x-ray fish

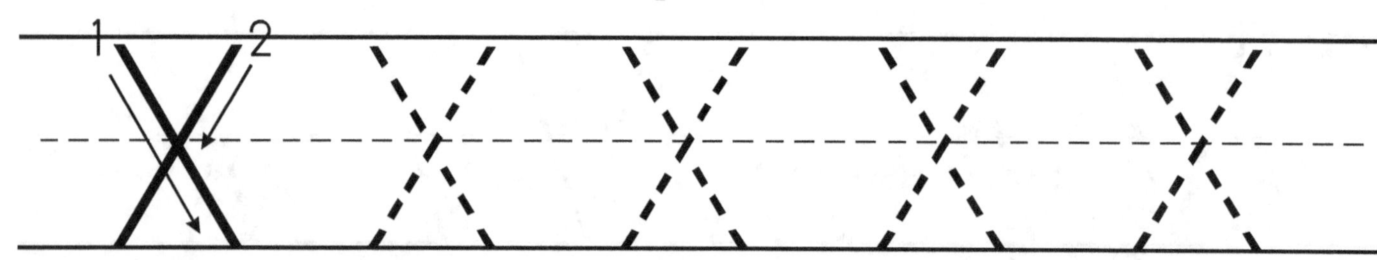

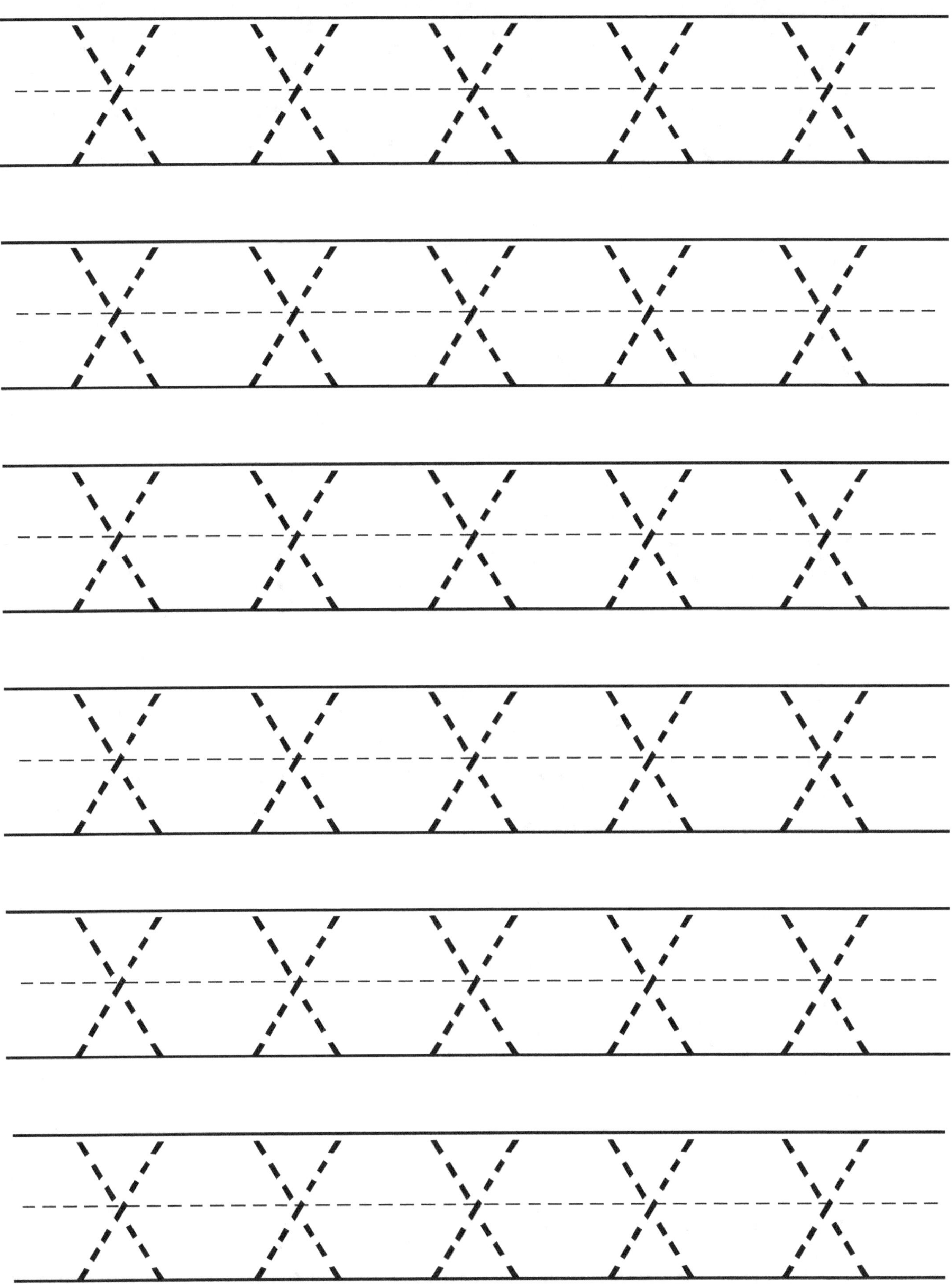

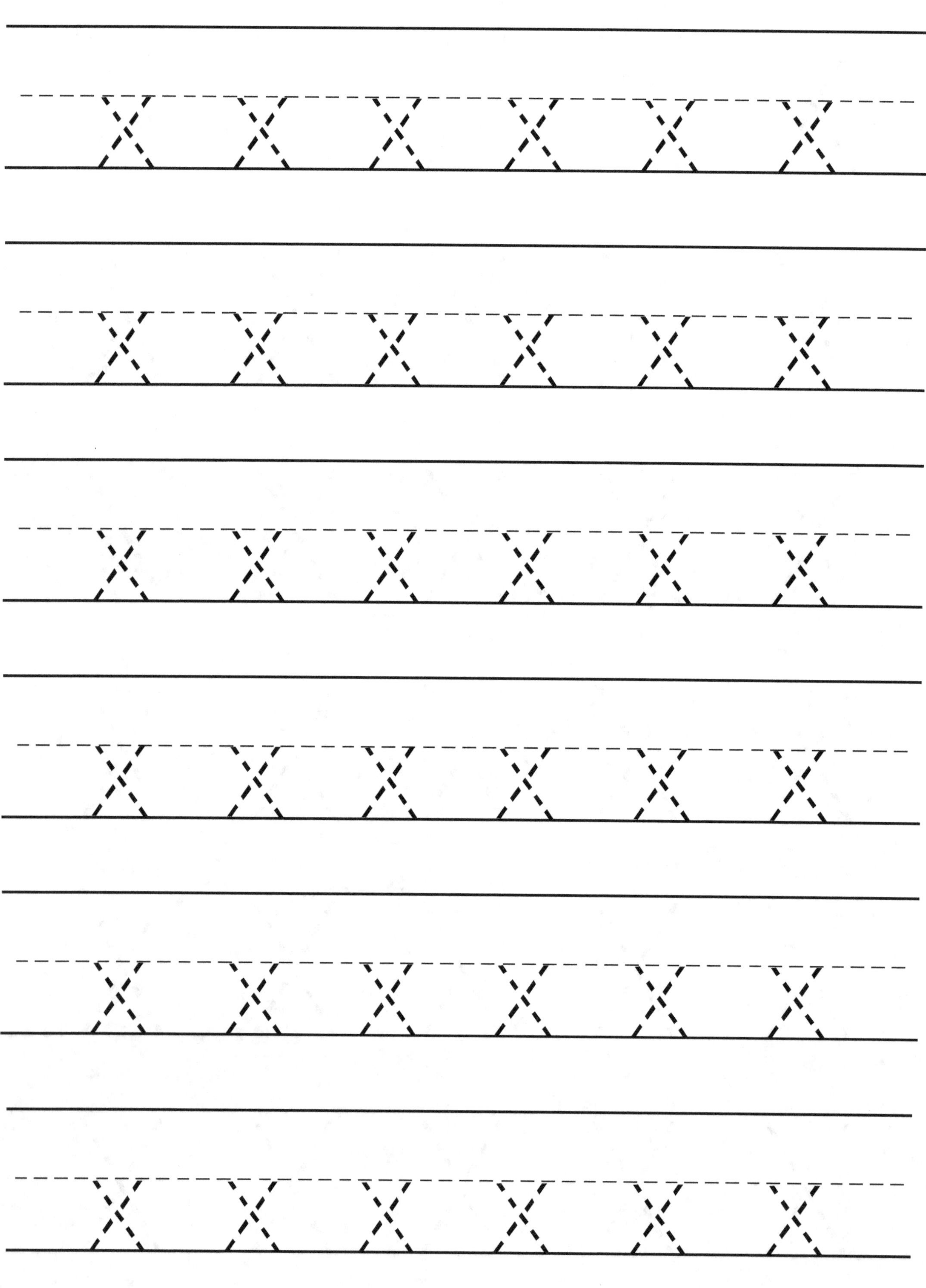

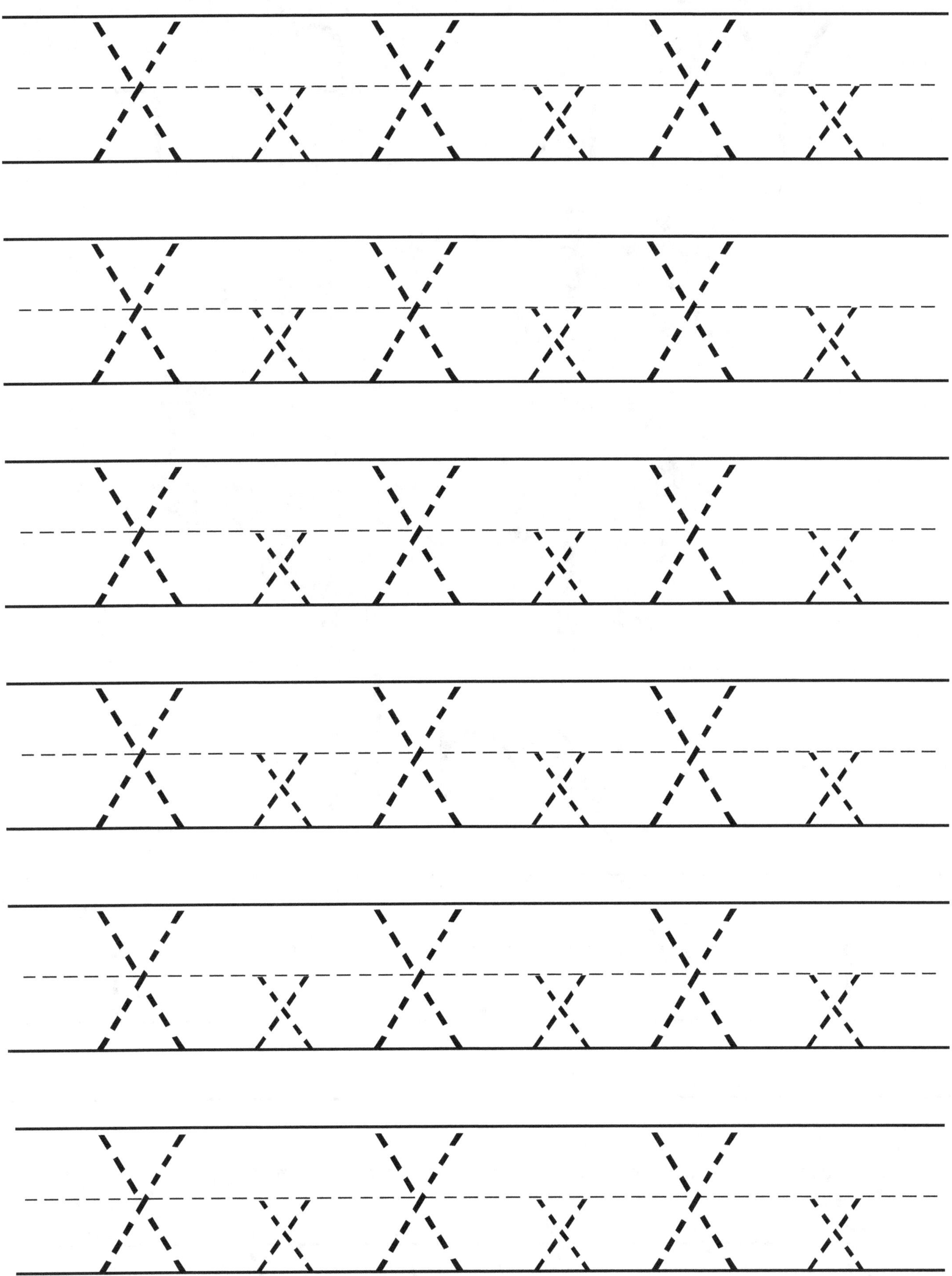

Y is for

yak

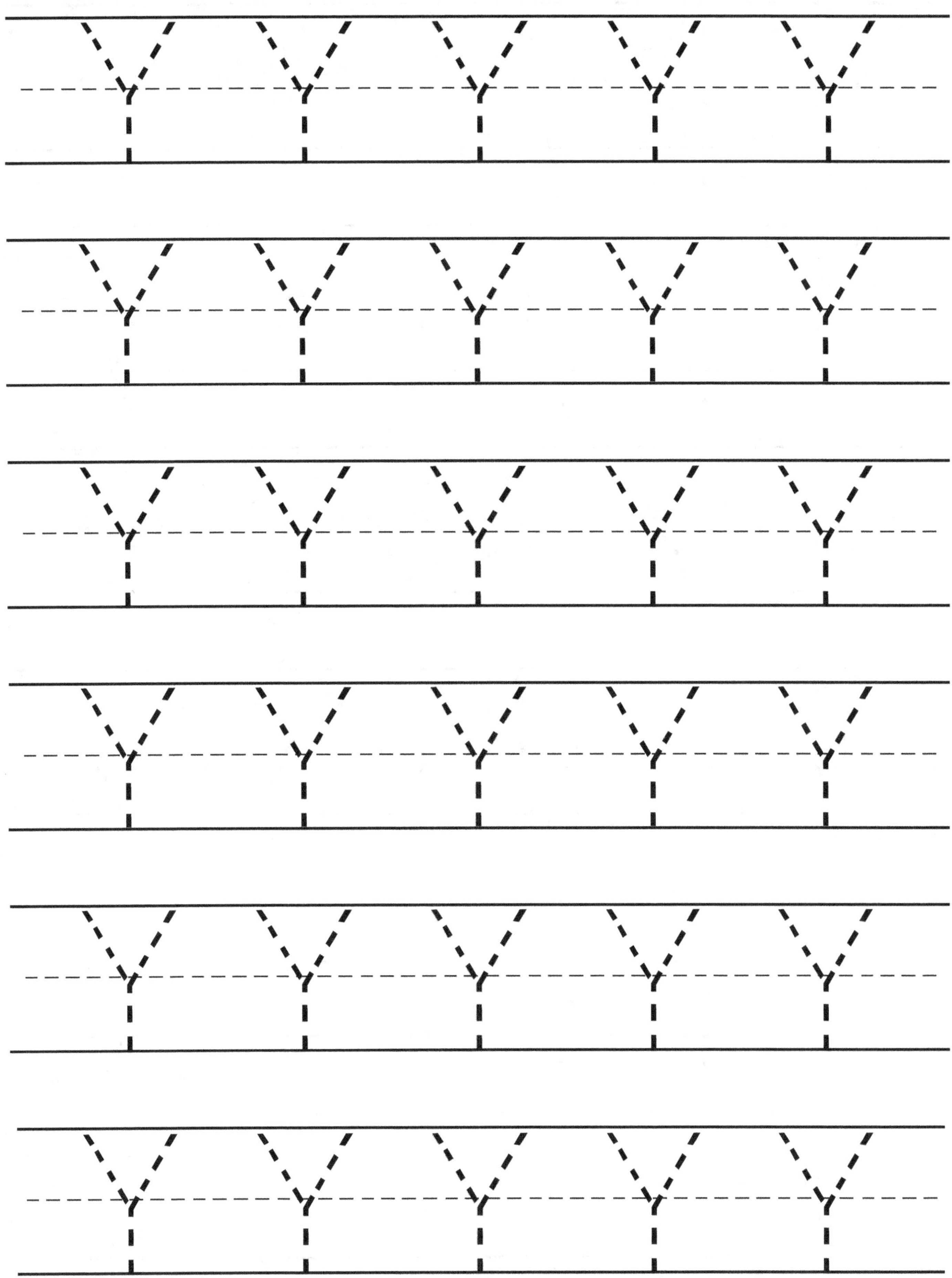

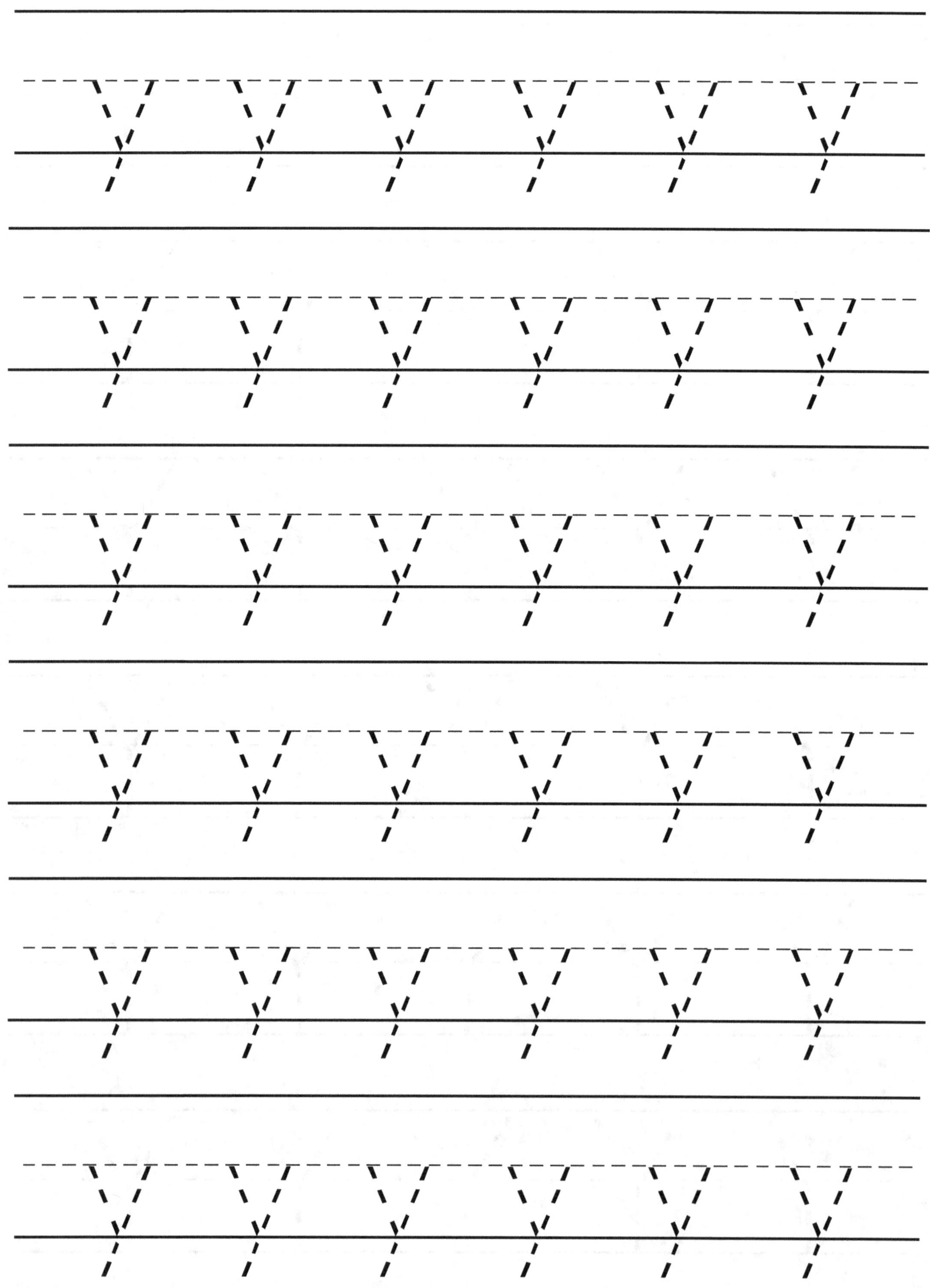

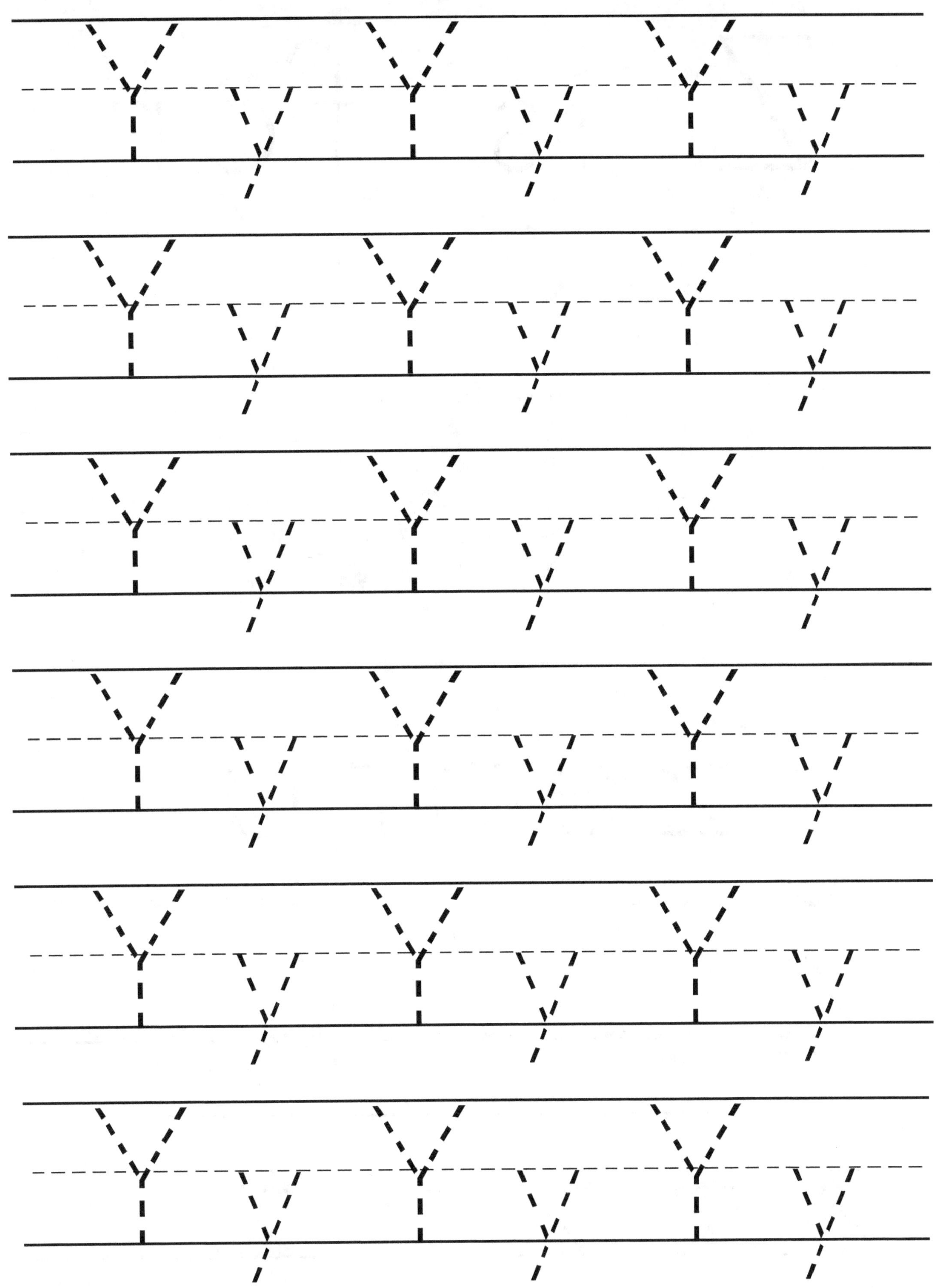

Z is for

zebra

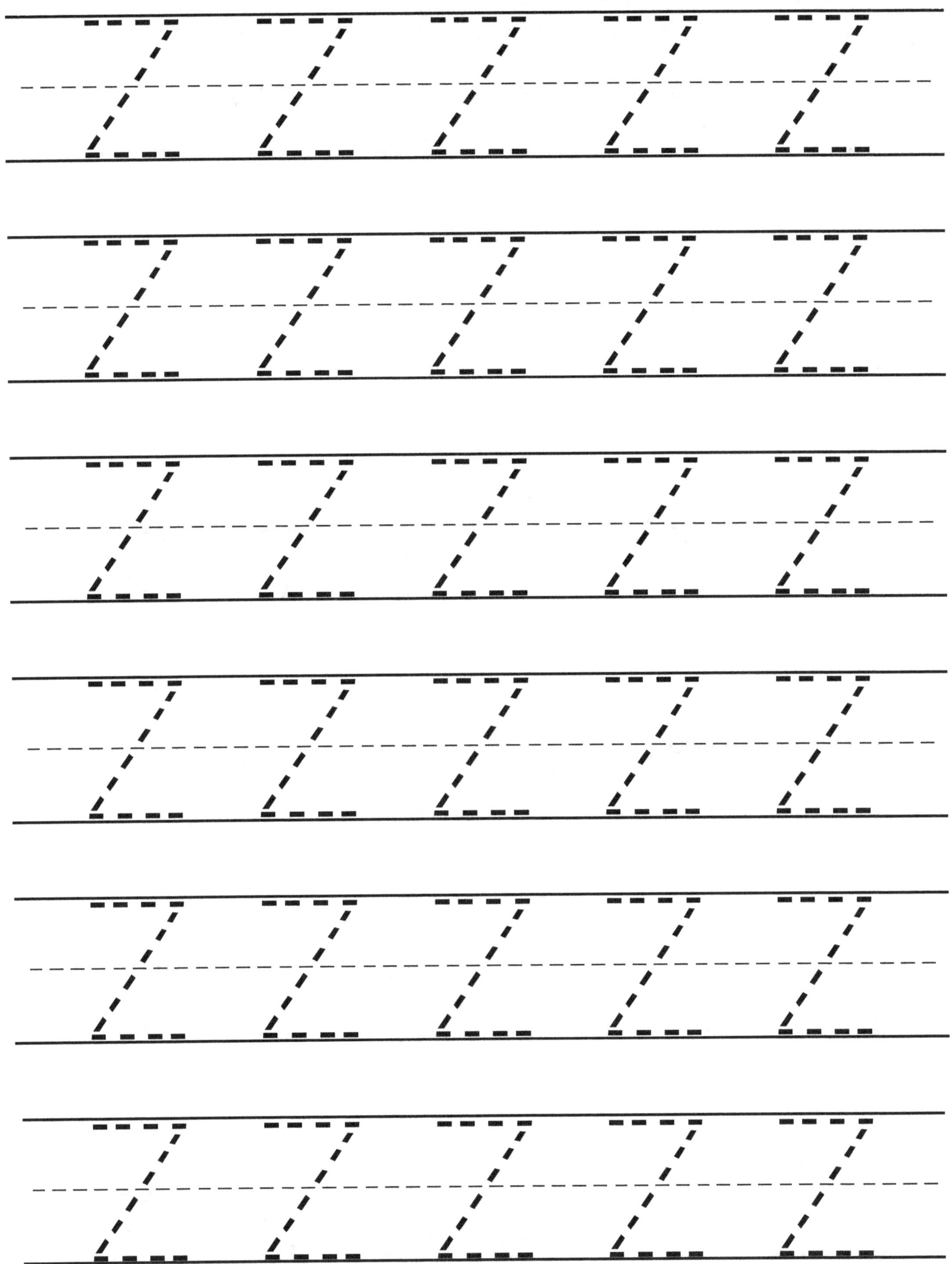

Z Z Z Z Z Z

Z Z Z Z Z Z

Z Z Z Z Z Z

Z Z Z Z Z Z

Z Z Z Z Z Z

Z Z Z Z Z Z

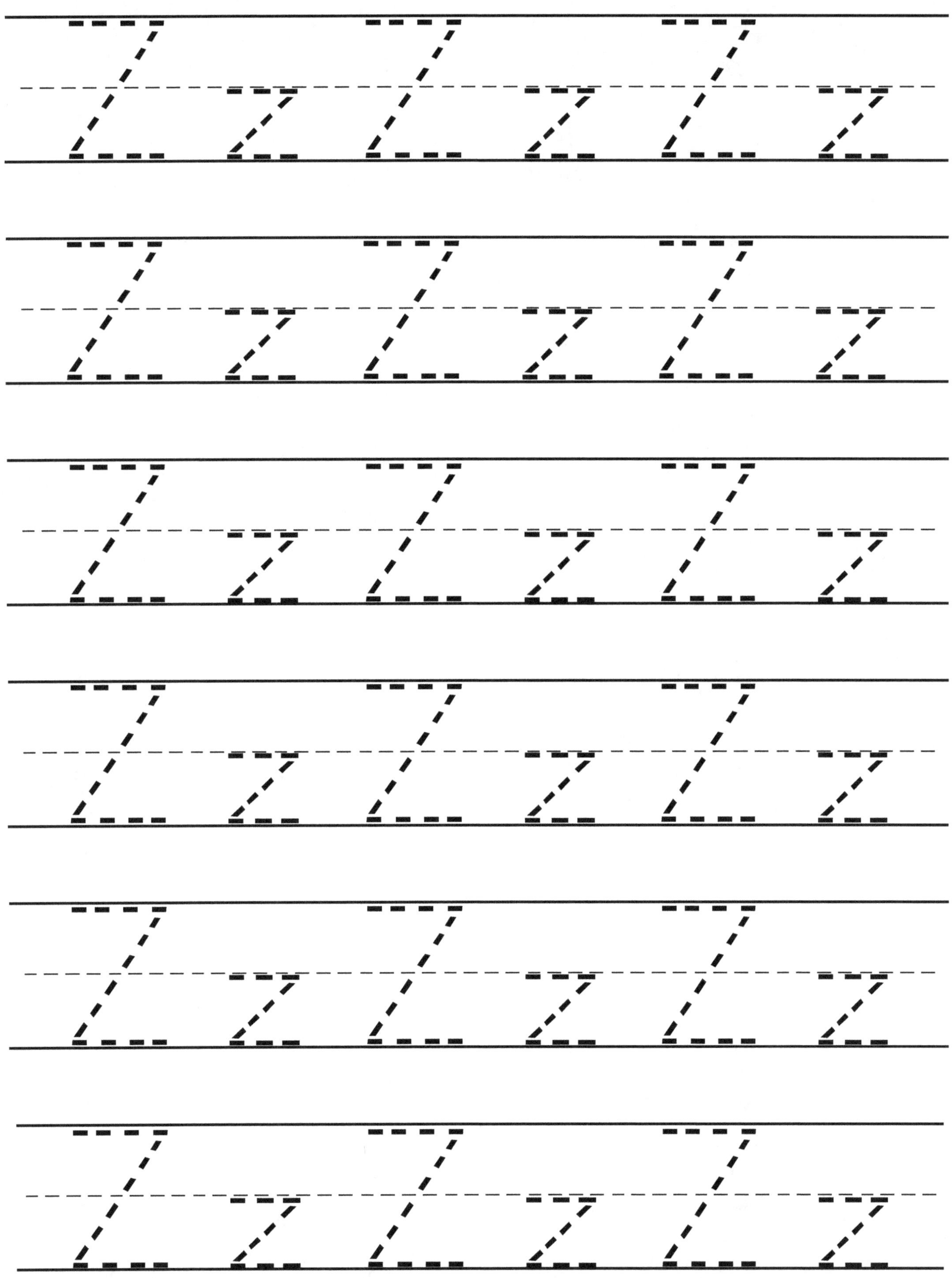

About the Author

Talia Knight is the pen name of the author/artist. She is a prolific reader, and when she was faced with the task of choosing a pen name, she knew just where to turn. She chose "Talia" because it's the name of one her favorite fantasy heroines, and "Knight" because she loves sword and sorcery fantasy.

Of course, once she had the name, she had to create a picture worthy of her new fantasy-inspired alter ego. What could be more appropriate than a strong female (she has to be strong—she's wearing all that armor!) trekking through the desert with perfect hair and absolutely no sweat dripping down her face? Her makeup isn't even smudged. Realistically, she ought to be laid out flat on that sand, red as a lobster with heatstroke.

On a more serious note, Talia considers herself the luckiest person in the world because she has the privilege of helping to care for her handicapped sister while living in the great state of Texas. When she's not spending time with her sister or playing with her many nieces and nephews, she's usually doing something with books. Creating, writing, editing, selling—you name it, she's probably done it.

Want FREE coloring pages?

Talia Knight is giving away a free coloring book

If you like <u>FREE</u>, you can download your coloring book here:

TranquilityColoring.com/harmony

ISBN-13: 978-1983640544   ISBN-10: 1983640549

Published by Tranquility Coloring
TranquilityColoring.com